C000069867

YOUR NEW
IDENTITY

VICTORYSERIES

STUDY **2**

YOUR NEW
IDENTITY

A TRANSFORMING UNION WITH GOD

NEIL T. ANDERSON

BETHANYHOUSE

a division of Baker Publishing Group

www.BethanyHouse.com

© 2014 by Neil T. Anderson

Published by Bethany House Publishers
11400 Hampshire Avenue South
Bloomington, Minnesota 55438
www.bethanyhouse.com

Bethany House Publishers is a division of
Baker Publishing Group, Grand Rapids, Michigan

Printed in the United States of America

All rights reserved. No part of this publication may be reproduced, stored in a retrieval system, or transmitted in any form or by any means—for example, electronic, photocopy, recording—without the prior written permission of the publisher. The only exception is brief quotations in printed reviews.

Library of Congress Cataloging-in-Publication Data is on file at the Library of Congress, Washington, DC.

ISBN 978-0-7642-1382-3

Unless otherwise indicated, Scripture quotations are from the HOLY BIBLE, NEW INTERNATIONAL VERSION®. Copyright © 1973, 1978, 1984 by Biblica, Inc.™ Used by permission of Zondervan. All rights reserved.

Scripture quotations identified ESV are from The Holy Bible, English Standard Version® (ESV®), copyright © 2001 by Crossway, a publishing ministry of Good News Publishers. Used by permission. All rights reserved. ESV Text Edition: 2007

Scripture quotations identified NASB are from the New American Standard Bible®, copyright © 1960, 1962, 1963, 1968, 1971, 1972, 1973, 1975, 1977, 1995 by The Lockman Foundation. Used by permission.

Scripture quotations identified NKJV are from the New King James Version. Copyright © 1982 by Thomas Nelson, Inc. Used by permission. All rights reserved.

Scripture quotations identified NLT are from the Holy Bible, New Living Translation, copyright © 1996, 2004, 2007 by Tyndale House Foundation. Used by permission of Tyndale House Publishers, Inc., Carol Stream, Illinois 60188. All rights reserved.

Cover design by Inside Out Design

14 15 16 17 18 19 20   7 6 5 4 3 2 1

Contents

Contents

Introduction

The Victory Series

It's the beginning of another busy day. We want to look nice and make a good impression, so we spend some time showering, combing our hair, putting on makeup, and all the other grooming routines. Those who are more physically disciplined will find time to exercise. We have a quick bite to eat and it's off to work, school, or play.

Natural disciplines such as these are important. If we didn't do these things, we would suffer the consequences—whether that would be getting in trouble with our boss, or being tardy for school, or angering a friend because we didn't show up for an appointment. The same is true of spiritual disciplines, though it is easier for us to overlook their value, because we don't always see the immediate benefits. Wondering what's in it for us seems so unrighteous, but there are no sure commitments with no sure rewards.

The apostle Paul addresses this issue when he instructs us, "Train yourself to be godly. For physical training is of some value, but godliness has value for all things, holding promise for both the present life and the life to come" (1 Timothy 4:7–8). In other words, spiritual disciplines are more profitable than physical disciplines. Our lives will be more fruitful if we spend time with the Lord and seek to be transformed by the renewing of our minds to the truth of His Word.

What you are holding in your hands is the second study in the VICTORY SERIES on how you can discover your new identity in Christ and become the person God created you to be. As you work through the six sessions in this Bible study, you will learn about the new life Christ has given to you, about God's nature and character, and about the relationship He wants to form with you. You will discover the new heart and new spirit God has placed within you and about the assurance of salvation you have received. There are seven more studies in the VICTORY SERIES that will provide a practical systematic theology by which to live. All eight studies cover the subjects listed in the following tables.

As a believer in Christ, you must first be rooted "in Him" so that you can be built up "in Him." Just as you encounter challenges as you grow physically, so too you will encounter hurdles as you grow spiritually. The following chart illustrates what obstacles you need to overcome and lessons you need to learn at various stages of growth spiritually, rationally, emotionally, volitionally, and relationally.

Levels of Conflict

	Level One Rooted in Christ	Level Two Built up in Christ	Level Three Living in Christ
Spiritual	Lack of salvation or assurance (Eph. 2:1–3)	Living according to the flesh (Gal. 5:19–21)	Insensitive to the Spirit's leading (Heb. 5:11–14)
Rational	Pride and ignorance (1 Cor. 8:1)	Wrong belief or philosophy (Col. 2:8)	Lack of knowledge (Hos. 4:6)
Emotional	Fearful, guilty, and shameful (Matt. 10:26–33; Rom. 3:23)	Angry, anxious, and depressed (Eph. 4:31; 1 Pet. 5:7; 2 Cor. 4:1–18)	Discouraged and sorrowful (Gal. 6:9)
Volitional	Rebellious (1 Tim. 1:9)	Lack of self-control (1 Cor. 3:1–3)	Undisciplined (2 Thess. 3:7, 11)
Relational	Rejected and unloved (1 Pet. 2:4)	Bitter and unforgiving (Col. 3:13)	Selfish (1 Cor. 10:24; Phil. 2:1–5)

This VICTORY SERIES will address these obstacles and hurdles and help you understand what it means to be firmly rooted in Christ, grow in Christ, live free in Christ, and overcome in Christ. The goal of the course is to help you attain greater levels of spiritual growth, as the following diagram illustrates:

Levels of Growth

	Level One	Level Two	Level Three
	Rooted in Christ	Built up in Christ	Living in Christ
Spiritual	Child of God (Rom. 8:16)	Lives according to the Spirit (Gal. 5:22–23)	Led by the Spirit (Rom. 8:14)
Rational	Knows the truth (John 8:32)	Correctly uses the Bible (2 Tim. 2:15)	Adequate and equipped (2 Tim. 3:16–17)
Emotional	Free (Gal. 5:1)	Joyful, peaceful, and patient (Gal. 5:22)	Contented (Phil. 4:11)
Volitional	Submissive (Rom. 13:1–5)	Self-controlled (Gal. 5:23)	Disciplined (1 Tim. 4:7–8)
Relational	Accepted and forgiven (Rom. 5:8; 15:7)	Forgiving (Eph. 4:32)	Loving and unselfish (Phil. 2:1–5)

Before starting each daily reading, review the portion of Scripture listed for that day, then complete the Bible study and application questions at the end of each day's reading. These questions have been written to allow you to reflect on the material and apply to your life the ideas presented in the reading. At the end of each study, I have included a quote from a Church father illustrating the continuity of the Christian faith. Featured articles will appear in the text throughout the series, which are for the edification of the reader and not necessarily meant for discussion.

If you are part of a small group, be prepared to share your thoughts and insights with your group. You may also want to set up an accountability partnership with someone in your group to encourage you to take on the challenge at the end of each session. For those of you who are leading a small group, there are leader tips at the end of this book that will help you guide your participants through the material.

As with any spiritual discipline, you will be tempted at times not to finish this study. There is a "sure reward" for those who make a "sure commitment." The VICTORY SERIES is far more than an intellectual exercise. The truth will not set you free if you only acknowledge it and discuss it on an intellectual level. For the truth to transform your life, you must believe it personally and allow it to sink deep into your heart. Trust the Holy Spirit to lead you into all truth and to enable you to be the person God has created you to be. Decide to live what you have chosen to believe.

Dr. Neil T. Anderson

A New Life "in Christ"

Who our heavenly Father is and who we are in Christ are the two most important beliefs that every Christian should possess. The following testimony illustrates why these beliefs are so critical:

My husband and I are missionaries. Even though I have been a Christian for 21 years, I never understood God's forgiveness and my spiritual heritage. I have been a bulimic for years. I began this horrible practice in Bible college. I never thought this living hell would ever end, and I would have killed myself had I not thought that it was a sin. I felt God had turned His back on me and I was doomed to hell because I couldn't overcome this sin. I felt like a failure, and I hated myself.

When I read Victory Over the Darkness *and began to understand who I was in Christ, it opened my eyes to God's truth and love. Today I feel like a new Christian. I can finally say I am free—free of Satan's bondage and aware of the lies with which he has been filling me. Before, I would confess to God and beg His forgiveness when I binged and purged. Yet the next time I fell deeper into Satan's grasp, because I couldn't forgive myself and I couldn't accept God's forgiveness. I always thought the answer was to draw closer to God, but I went to Him in fear and confusion.*

No more! I don't consider myself a bulimic. I consider myself Christ's friend and a forgiven child of God. Food has no power over me. Satan has lost his grip on me!

Daily Readings

1. A New Identity "in Christ"	Genesis 32:1–32
2. A New Position "in Christ"	Colossians 2:1–10
3. Crucified "in Christ"	Galatians 2:11–20
4. A New Person "in Christ"	Colossians 3:1–10
5. We Are Now Saints "in Christ"	1 Timothy 1:12–17

1

A New Identity "in Christ"

Genesis 32:1–32

Key Point

When we encounter God, He frees us from our past and gives us a new identity.

Key Verse

Therefore, if anyone is in Christ, the new creation has come: The old has gone, the new is here!

2 Corinthians 5:17

Jacob was in a difficult situation. Twenty years before he had tricked his father, Isaac, into giving him a blessing due to his older brother, Esau. Esau was furious and vowed revenge (see Genesis 27). Jacob fled for his life, but he realized he could not avoid Esau forever. So he sent messengers to Esau's land with a message of reconciliation. Esau came to meet him—with 400 men.

Jacob's name literally meant "supplanter," and he had lived up to that identity. As he waited for Esau beside the Jordan River, a "man" appeared and wrestled with him, and Jacob struggled to get away. Suddenly, the dawn broke, and Jacob saw the face of God. The whole battle changed, and Jacob struggled to hang on. He wouldn't let go until this "man" blessed him. This encounter with God forever changed Jacob: "Your name will no longer be Jacob, but Israel, because you have struggled with God and with humans and have overcome" (Genesis 32:28). Jacob limped across the Jordan, but his name was now Israel, which means "God strives."

Our encounter with God has forever changed us. We are no longer by nature objects of wrath (see Ephesians 2:3); we are children of God (see 1 John 3:1–3). "For you were once darkness, but now you are light in the Lord. Live as children of light" (Ephesians 5:8). First Peter 2:9–10 states, "You are a chosen people, a royal priesthood, a holy nation, God's special possession, that you may declare the praises of him who called you out of darkness into his wonderful light. Once you were not a people, but now you are the people of God; once you had not received mercy, but now you have received mercy."

Everyone has struggled with his or her self-perception. Little children have a natural heritage and identity, which they received from their earthly parents. Teenagers begin to search for their own identity. Adults try to make a name for themselves in the world. The natural tendency is for them to find their identity in the things they do, the places they live, and the roles they play.

It is totally different for believers who have become new creations in Christ. "Here there is no Gentile or Jew, circumcised or uncircumcised, barbarian, Scythian, slave or free, but Christ is all, and is in all" (Colossians 3:11). In other words, there are no racial, religious, cultural, or social distinctions. All believers are children of God and share the same status in the family of God.

Paul says, "From now on we regard no one from a worldly point of view" (2 Corinthians 5:16). Literally, this means that Paul no longer recognizes believers according to the flesh—that is, their natural identity or who they were in Adam. He recognizes believers as new creations in Christ (see 2 Corinthians 5:17).

Paul asks, "Don't you know that all of us who were baptized into Christ Jesus were baptized into his death?" (Romans 6:3). Don't you know that we have been united with Christ in His death and resurrection (see verse 5)?

Don't you know who you are? You must keep asking yourself until you reply, "Yes, I do know who I am: a new person in Christ, and by the grace of God I shall live accordingly."

How and why did Jacob's behavior change when his perception of the "stranger" changed?

_____

_____

_____

From where do natural people derive their identity?

_____

_____

_____

How does God's perception of us change after we are born again?

_____

_____

_____

How have you perceived yourself in the past? How has that perception changed since you became a Christian?

_____

_____

_____

_____

How has your perception about yourself and God affected the way you live?

_____

_____

_____

Even if believers are still in their earthly bodies, we do not relate to them that way, because the life according to the flesh has been transcended. We have been born again by the Spirit and have learned a different kind of behavior, which is that of heaven. It is Christ who has brought about this change. There was a time when we knew Him in His earthly life, but now we know Him in the perfection of His resurrection.

John Chrysostom (AD 347–407)

In Christ You Are:

The salt of the earth (Matthew 5:13).

The light of the world (Matthew 5:14).

A child of God (John 1:12).

A part of the true vine, a channel of Christ's life (John 15:1, 5).

Christ's friend (John 15:15).

Chosen and appointed by Christ to bear His fruit (John 15:16).

A slave of righteousness (Romans 6:18).

Enslaved to God (Romans 6:22).

A child of God; God is spiritually your Father (Romans 8:14–15).

A joint heir with Christ, sharing His inheritance with Him (Romans 8:17).

A temple—a dwelling place—of God. His Spirit and His life dwell in you (1 Corinthians 3:16; 6:19).

United to the Lord and one spirit with Him (1 Corinthians 6:17).

A member of Christ's Body (1 Corinthians 12:27; Ephesians 5:30).

A new creation in Christ (2 Corinthians 5:17).

Reconciled to God and a minister of reconciliation (2 Corinthians 5:18–19).

A son of God and one in Christ (Galatians 3:26, 28).

An heir of God, since you are a son of God (Galatians 4:6–7).

A saint (Ephesians 1:1; 1 Corinthians 1:2; Philippians 1:1; Colossians 1:2).

God's workmanship—His handiwork—born anew in Christ to do His work (Ephesians 2:10).

A fellow citizen with the rest of God's family (Ephesians 2:19).

A prisoner of Christ (Ephesians 3:1; 4:1).

Righteous and holy (Ephesians 4:24).

A citizen of heaven, seated in heaven right now (Philippians 3:20; Ephesians 2:6).

Hidden with Christ in God (Colossians 3:3).

An expression of the life of Christ because He is your life (Colossians 3:4).

Chosen of God, holy and dearly loved (Colossians 3:12; 1 Thessalonians 1:4).

A son of light and not of darkness (1 Thessalonians 5:5).

A holy partaker of a heavenly calling (Hebrews 3:1).

A partaker of Christ; you share in His life (Hebrews 3:14).

One of God's living stones, being built up in Christ as a spiritual house (1 Peter 2:5).

A member of a chosen race, a royal priesthood, a holy nation, and a people for God's own possession (1 Peter 2:9–10).

An alien and stranger to this world in which you temporarily live (1 Peter 2:11).

An enemy of the devil (1 Peter 5:8).

A child of God and will resemble Christ when He returns (1 John 3:1–2).

Born of God, and the evil one cannot touch you (1 John 5:18).

Not the great "I AM" (Exodus 3:14; John 8:24, 28, 58), but by the grace of God, you are what you are (1 Corinthians 15:10).

2

A New Position "in Christ"

Colossians 2:1–10

Key Point

Being alive "in Christ" is the basis for every aspect of the Christian life.

Key Verse

Now if we are children, then we are heirs—heirs of God and co-heirs with Christ.

Romans 8:17

The Christian's new identity is based on his or her position "in Christ." The prepositional phrase "in Christ," "in Him," or "in the beloved" is one of the most often-used expressions in the Epistles. The phrase occurs 40 times in the book of Ephesians alone. It means that our souls are in union with God. For every verse stating that Christ is in us (see Colossians 1:27), there are 10 verses stating that we are "in Christ." "In Christ" we are called to salvation (see 1 Corinthians 7:22), regenerated (see Ephesians 1:3; 2:10), and justified (see Romans 8:1–2). "In Christ" we die (see 1 Thessalonians 4:16), and "in Him" our bodies will be raised up again (see 1 Corinthians 15:22).

Every step in becoming more like Jesus is made possible because we are spiritually alive "in Christ." We are to be firmly rooted "in Him" in order to be built up "in Him," which makes it possible to live "in Him" (Colossians 2:6–7). This dependency and union with God is Paul's explanation for how we can live the Christian life. In sending Timothy to Corinth, Paul said, "He will remind you of my way of life *in Christ Jesus*, which agrees with what I teach everywhere in every church" (1 Corinthians 4:17, emphasis added).

"God has given us eternal life, and this life is *in his Son*" (1 John 5:11, emphasis added). Paul speaks of "the promise of life that is *in Christ Jesus*" (2 Timothy 1:1, emphasis added). "*In Christ*" are "faith and love" (1 Timothy 1:14), "grace" (2 Timothy 2:1), "salvation" (verse 10), "all the treasures of wisdom and knowledge" (Colossians 2:3), and God's "riches" (Philippians 4:19). Paul says that it is because of God's work that Christians are "*in Christ Jesus*, who has become for us wisdom from God—that is, our righteousness, holiness and redemption" (1 Corinthians 1:30, emphasis added).

With our identity in Christ come the blessings that Christ alone has merited. "Now if we are children, then we are heirs—heirs of God and co-heirs with Christ" (Romans 8:17). Further, "If you belong to Christ, then you are Abraham's seed, and heirs according to the promise" (Galatians 3:29). "For in Christ all the fullness of the Deity lives in bodily form, and in Christ you have been brought to fullness. He is the head over every power and authority" (Colossians 2:9–10).

Notice that the phrase "have been brought" is past tense. We were incomplete without Christ, but now we have been made complete (fullness). As believers, we are not trying to become children of God; rather, we are already children of God who are in the process of becoming like Christ. Now that we are complete in Christ, the goal is to proclaim Jesus, "admonishing and teaching everyone with all wisdom, so that we may present everyone fully mature in Christ" (Colossians 1:28).

Paul contrasts the means by which we grow in Christ with the human traditions of the world. "See to it that no one takes you captive through hollow and deceptive philosophy, which depends on human tradition and the elemental spiritual forces of this world rather than on Christ" (Colossians 2:8). All the humanistic wisdom of this world cannot reproduce in us what only the life of Christ can. Paul says, "I can do everything *through him* who gives me strength" (Philippians 4:13, emphasis added); and Jesus tells us, "Apart from me you can do nothing" (John 15:5).

Why is it so important to know who we are "in Christ"?

_____

_____

_____

Ephesians 1 describes the believer's incredible position in Christ. Count how many times the prepositional phrase "in Christ" or "in Him" occurs in just that one chapter. What does that tell you?

_____

_____

_____

How can the Church keep from being deceived by "fine-sounding arguments" (Colossians 2:4) and "hollow and deceptive philosophy, which depends on human tradition and the elemental spiritual forces of this world rather than on Christ" (verse 8)?

_____

_____

_____

_____

What does your position in Christ mean to you on a daily basis?

_____

_____

_____

How can the reality of being rooted in Christ strengthen you to become more like Him?

_____

_____

_____

Since it was impossible that our life, which had been estranged from God, should of itself return to the high and heavenly place, for this reason, as the apostle says, He who knew no sin is made sin for us and frees us from the curse by taking on Him our curse as His own.

Gregory of Nyssa (AD 330–395)

3

Crucified "in Christ"

Galatians 2:11–20

Key Point

The eternal life we have in Christ sets us free from the power of sin and death.

Key Verse

The life I now live in the body, I live by faith in the Son of God, who loved me and gave himself for me.

Galatians 2:20

Paul said, "I died to the law" (Galatians 2:19) because "I have been crucified with Christ and I no longer live, but Christ lives in me" (verse 20). This is possible because of our union with God. As believers we are no longer "in Adam" but "in Christ." Paul identified every believer with Christ in His death (see Romans 6:3, 6; Colossians 3:1–3), in His burial (see Romans 6:4), in His resurrection (see Romans 6:5, 8, 11), in His ascension (see Ephesians 2:6), in His life (see Romans 6:10–11), in

His power (see Ephesians 1:19–20), and in His inheritance (see Romans 8:16–17; Ephesians 1:11–14).

When Paul said, "I have been crucified with Christ" (Galatians 2:20), he literally meant, "I have been and continue to be crucified with Christ." The eternal life we received at salvation was the eternal life of Christ, which included eternity past and eternity future. We are identified with every aspect of Christ's eternal life because we are united with Him. Because we are eternally connected to God, we can be crucified with Christ and at the same time be seated with Him in the heavenly realms (see Ephesians 2:6). It is impossible for the finite mind to fully grasp the idea of eternity, but that is our reality.

Before we came to Christ, we were under the law and in bondage to sin, which only leads to death. We had to be crucified with Christ "so that the body of sin might be done away with" (Romans 6:6 NKJV). The "body of sin" refers to the person or self (living in bodily form) under the law and the rule of sin. This person was "done away with" by being crucified with Christ. The Greek term "done away with" can mean "rendered ineffective or powerless," "destroyed," "brought to an end," or "released from." Our old self was in bondage to sin and its mastery. That old self has died with Christ. Now a new self exists, which is no longer under the mastery of sin.

Sin reigns through death; therefore, the way to freedom from sin is through death (see Romans 6:6). For this reason, if a person dies to sin, sin loses its mastery over that person. Because the believer has died with Christ (participated with Him in His death to sin), that believer is free from the mastery of sin and lives a new life of freedom from the law of sin and death (see Romans 8:1–2). Paul expresses this new freedom from sin in Romans 6:19–20, 22: "Just as you used to offer yourselves as slaves to impurity and to ever-increasing wickedness, so now offer yourselves as slaves to righteousness leading to holiness. When you were slaves to sin, you were free from the control of righteousness. . . . But now that you have been set free from sin and have become slaves of God, the benefit you reap leads to holiness, and the result is eternal life."

Death is the end of a relationship, but not the end of existence. According to Paul, we should consider ourselves to be alive in Christ and dead to sin (see Romans 6:11). Physical death is still imminent, but we shall continue to live spiritually even if we die physically. Sin is still present and appealing, but we don't have to yield to it. The eternal life of Christ within us is our victory.

How can we say that we have been "crucified with Christ"?

_____

_____

_____

What are we putting to death when we are crucified with Christ?

_____

_____

_____

How are we set free from sin? How does sin lose its mastery over us?

_____

_____

_____

_____

How would it affect the way you lived if you fully believed that you were free from the power of sin?

_____

_____

_____

_____

You have been crucified with Christ and raised with Christ. The first dealt with sin and the other the consequence of sin. What hope does that give you for the future?

Not I, who once ate from the earth. Not I, who once was grass, as all flesh is grass, but Christ who lives in me. That is, there lives that living bread which comes from heaven, there lives wisdom, there lives righteousness, there lives the resurrection.

Ambrose (AD 340–397)

4

A New Person "in Christ"

Colossians 3:1–10

Key Point

We must lay aside our former way of life and embrace the new life we have in Christ.

Key Verse

For all of you who were baptized into Christ have clothed yourselves with Christ.

Galatians 3:27

In Romans 6:6, Paul wrote that our old self was crucified with Christ. This was a decisive and definite act in our past. In Colossians 3:9–10, Paul exhorts us to stop living in the old sins of our past life: "Since you have taken off your old self with its practices and have put on the new self." Paul makes a similar point in Ephesians 4:22, 24: "You were taught, with regard to your former way of life, to put off your old self . . . and to put on the new self, created to be like God in true righteousness and holiness."

In Romans 6:6 and Colossians 3:9–10, Paul clearly teaches a definitive *past* action, which happened the moment we were born again. However, the Ephesians passage implies a *continuous* action on our part. The old self was crucified with Christ (positional sanctification), but as believers we have to do our part in putting off the old self and putting on the new self (progressive sanctification). This is not an exhortation to do again for ourselves what Christ has already done; rather, Paul is saying that we are new people in Christ who must become in practice what God has already made us. We must have the resolve to not let our "former way of life" impinge on who we are now.

In Galatians 3:27, Paul says, "For all of you who were baptized into Christ have clothed yourselves with Christ." The term "clothed yourselves" is the same word translated as "put on" in the above passages. It means that we are to "put on Christ." To clothe yourself with or to put on a person means to take on the characteristics of that individual and become like him or her. Paul says that we are to "clothe ourselves with the Lord Jesus Christ" (Romans 13:14). This spiritual transformation has a decisive beginning, but it is not final or complete. The process of putting off the old self who was in Adam and putting on the new self who is in Christ is the sanctifying process that makes real in our experience what has already happened at salvation. In other words, we are to become by God's grace the people He has already made us.

The transformation of a caterpillar illustrates this spiritual metamorphosis. This earthbound creature is led by instinct to climb as high as it can by its own strength—usually onto the limb of a tree. There it sows a little button that forms an attachment for the cocoon it spins around itself as it hangs upside down. The caterpillar then ceases to exist, and a miraculous transformation takes place. The caterpillar has "crucified" itself in order to be "resurrected" a butterfly. The caterpillar gave up all that it was in order to become all that the Creator designed it to be.

The caterpillar can't take any credit for becoming a butterfly any more than we can take credit for the work of Christ, which is imputed to us by the grace of God. Imagine what would happen to the growth of the new butterfly if it chose to believe that it was still a caterpillar and kept on crawling instead of flying. The butterfly would never reach its potential.

Neither will we if we fail to put aside the old self and embrace our new life in Christ.

Review Colossians 3:1–10. Because we have been "raised with Christ," on what are we to set our hearts and minds? How do we do that practically in our daily lives?

How is putting our old self to death both a past action and a continuous action?

What does it mean to "clothe" yourself with Christ? What spiritual transformation occurs when you do this?

What part of your former life do you need to put off?

In what ways are you still living like a caterpillar instead of like a butterfly?

_____

_____

_____

The "old self" includes all born as earthly men in their old nature. It is this "old self," this ancient condition of humanity, that is put off in Christ. Although his body continues, he nonetheless undergoes a change to new life engendered by living baptism. What he was has been "put off." His old life is renewed by the Holy water and the copious mercy of the anointing. He becomes new rather than old, whole rather than corrupt, fresh rather than enfeebled, an infant rather than an old man, eternal rather than ephemeral.

Origen (AD 184–253)

5

We Are Now Saints "in Christ"

1 Timothy 1:12–17

Key Point

A "saint" is someone who is united to Christ and has the capacity to overcome sin.

Key Verses

Dear friends, now we are children of God. . . . All who have this hope in him purify themselves, just as he is pure.

1 John 3:2–3

Believers are "called to be saints" (Romans 1:7 NKJV). Being a saint is part of God's calling. Notice that Paul writes "to the saints" in Ephesus (see Ephesians 1:1) and Philippi (see Philippians 1:1). Saints are not necessarily those who have earned such a lofty title by living an exemplary life or achieving a certain level of maturity. In the Bible, all believers are described as "saints," which means "holy ones" (see 1 Corinthians 1:2; 2 Corinthians 1:1).

Being a saint does not necessarily reflect any present measure of growth in character. Saints are those who are rightly related to God. In Scripture, believers are called "saints," "holy ones," or "righteous ones" more than 200 times. In contrast, unbelievers are called "sinners," "children of wrath," and "unrighteous ones" more than 300 times. Clearly, the term "saint" is used in Scripture to refer to the believer and "sinner" is used to refer to an unbeliever.

Although the New Testament teaches that believers can and do sin, it never clearly identifies the believer as a "sinner." However, Paul's reference to himself as "the worst of sinners" (1 Timothy 1:16) seems to contradict this teaching. Despite the use of the present tense by the apostle, Paul is actually referring to his pre-conversion opposition to the gospel.

First, Paul's reference to himself as a "sinner" is in support of the first half of the verse, "Christ Jesus came into the world to save sinners" (verse 15). The reference to "the ungodly and sinful" a few verses earlier (verse 9), along with the other New Testament uses of the term "sinners" for those who are outside salvation, shows that the "sinners" whom Christ came to save were outside of salvation.

Second, Paul immediately follows his reference to himself as a "sinner" by the statement, "But for that very reason I was shown [past tense] mercy" (1 Timothy 1:16). This clearly points to the past occasion of his conversion. Paul, the worst of sinners, uses himself as an example of God's unlimited patience. Because of his past action, Paul considered himself unworthy of what by God's grace and mercy he presently was: an apostle who was in no respect "inferior to the 'super-apostles'" (2 Corinthians 12:11).

Third, although Paul declares that he was the "worst" sinner, at the same time he declares that Christ had strengthened him for the ministry, having considered him faithful and trustworthy for the ministry to which he was called (see 1 Timothy 1:12). The term "sinner," therefore, does not describe Paul as a believer but rather is used in remembrance of what he was before Christ took hold of him.

As believers, we are not trying to become saints; we are saints who are becoming like Christ. Being saints is part of our positional sanctification. In no way does this deny the continuous struggle with sin. Christians can choose to sin, and many are dominated by the flesh and deceived by the

31

devil. Because believers sin, we want to call them sinners, but what we do does not determine who we are. Telling Christians they are sinners and then disciplining them if they don't act like saints is counterproductive at best and inconsistent with the Bible at worst. Believing who we really are in Christ determines what we do.

Why is it impossible for Christians to become "saints" through their own effort?

_____

_____

_____

What does being a "saint" imply? What does it *not* imply?

_____

_____

_____

Since the Epistles always identify believers for who they are in Christ, why is it counterproductive to label ourselves and others by who we were in the flesh?

_____

_____

_____

What labels have you placed on yourself that are counterproductive to your growth?

_____

_____

_____

How can seeing yourself from God's perspective alter your sense of worth and change how you live?

_____

_____

_____

He [Paul] writes to the saints in his customary manner [Philippians 1:1], but his intent is to write to those who are "saints in Christ Jesus," specifically those who confess that He is divine and human. . . . He is not writing to those who by their own deceptions suppress the truth.

Ambrosiaster (written c. AD 366–384)

Prayer and Praise

If you saw a giant man a mile away, he wouldn't look very big. But if you were standing right in front of him, you couldn't help but praise him. You wouldn't say, "Praise you!" You would say, or at least think, *My, you sure are big*! You would describe his dominant features. Worship is ascribing to God His divine attributes. It would not naturally flow from you if you were unaware of God's presence and you thought He was far off. But if you were suddenly ushered into God's glorious presence, you would immediately and voluntarily burst forth in praise—"beautiful, awesome, big, loving, kind, powerful!" In fact, there are no words that can adequately describe His majesty.

When we practice God's presence, worshiping Him is as natural a process as it was for David (see Psalm 138). When we get entangled in the daily affairs of life, it is easy to lose a conscious sense of His presence. That is when we need to worship God the most. God is seeking those who will worship Him in Spirit and in truth (see John 4:23), but not because He needs us to tell Him who He is. He is fully secure within Himself. We need to worship God because we need to keep the divine attributes of God continuously in our minds. There will be times in our Christian experience when we don't sense His presence. During these times, we need to continue believing that He is omnipresent, omnipotent, omniscient, and our loving heavenly Father.

When David prayed, God answered him. Being aware of God's presence made him bold and stouthearted (see Psalm 138:3). An awareness of God's presence and an acknowledgement of who He is are essential prerequisites for prayer. Jesus taught us how to approach God in the Lord's Prayer (Matthew 6:9–13). First, saying, "Our Father in heaven" (verse 9) implies that we have a relationship with Him. As children of God, we have the right to petition our heavenly Father. The crucifixion and resurrection of Christ made access to God possible.

Second, saying, "Hallowed be your name" (verse 9) is an act of praise. It is an acknowledgment that God is holy. You approach a judge in a court of law by saying, "your honor." If you show disrespect, you can be held for contempt and thrown out of court. We approach God with even greater respect. The throne of God is the ultimate authority of the universe, and there is no other judge remotely like Him in glory and majesty.

Third, saying, "Your kingdom come, your will be done, on earth as it is in heaven" (verse 10) means that His kingdom plans and priorities supersede ours. We try to ascertain God's will in prayer. We don't try to convince Him of our will. It is His kingdom we are trying to build, not ours.

Fourth, "Give us this day our daily bread" (verse 11) is a petition for real needs, not selfish wants.

A New Understanding of God's Character

Two children were granted an audience with the King. He had the power to give and take away from His subjects. Many feared His wrath and chose to keep their distance. Others wanted to gain His favor to enhance their status and profit from His wealth. A few naysayers didn't even believe He existed and chose to live as though He didn't.

The children sought counsel from others. What should they say in His presence? How should they address Him? Some said the children had an opportunity to influence the King, and they could suggest better ways for Him to rule. Others said the King had the power to make them prosperous if they gained His favor. Some cautioned them to keep their distance, lest the wrath of the King fall on them.

One child compiled a list of petitions, including some small favors for himself. When his time came to address the King, he shared his list. The

King listened intently. When asked how the audience went, the child said, "I think it went well. I hope to see Him again, because I have a few more items on my mind."

The other child came with a mixture of fear and wonder. Who was this ruler who had such power? What relationship could he possibly have with Him? The child had no fixed agenda. He marveled at the splendor of the palace. When he saw the King, he couldn't contain himself. Words of praise burst from his mouth, and he fell on his face in His presence. He felt so insignificant and unworthy to be in such a place. The King leaned over and gently lifted his head, and the child looked into the face of pure love.

When asked how his audience went with the King, the child said, "I am going to spend the rest of my life getting to know Him and learning how to serve Him to the best of my ability. I have heard so many false rumors about Him, but He is the King of kings. He is full of joy and wants all His subjects to come into His presence. They are like children to Him, and He loves every one of them."

Daily Readings

1. God Is Loving and Compassionate	Nehemiah 9:16–21
2. God Is Merciful and Good	Psalm 100:1–5
3. God Is Gracious and Kind	Hebrews 4:14–16
4. God Is Faithful	Psalm 89:1–52
5. God Is Immutable	Numbers 23:13–20

1

God Is Loving and Compassionate

Nehemiah 9:16–21

Key Point

God loves us because it is His nature to love, and that is why His love is unconditional.

Key Verse

But you are a forgiving God, gracious and compassionate, slow to anger and abounding in love.

Nehemiah 9:17

Whether or not there is a God is not the burning question on most people's minds. There are very few atheists who don't believe in God, but there are many who believe that His existence has little or no impact on how they live. "What difference does it make if there is a God?" and "Does He really care?" are the primary questions these people are asking. Those who have no personal relationship with God usually have a distorted concept of Him, and sadly, so do many who profess to believe in Him.

The truth about God is that He is compassionate and patient with us. Nehemiah testifies to this reality as he recalls the time when Aaron got tired of waiting for Moses to return from the mountain, so he and others created their own god by building a golden calf (see Exodus 32:1–6; Nehemiah 9:18). Even in their rebellion, God did not desert them. Nehemiah praised Him for this: "But you are a forgiving God, gracious and compassionate, slow to anger and abounding in love" (verse 17).

"And so we know and rely on the love God has for us. God is love. Whoever lives in love lives in God, and God in them" (1 John 4:16). The reason God loves us is because God *is* love. It is His nature to love us, and that is why His love is unconditional. God's love (*agape*) is not dependent on the object, which sets it apart from brotherly love (*phileo*).

It is natural to love those who love us, but it is divine to love those who don't. Jesus said, "If you love those who love you, what credit is that to you? Even sinners love those who love them. . . . But love your enemies, do good to them, and lend to them without expecting to get anything back. Then your reward will be great, and you will be children of the Most High, because he is kind to the ungrateful and wicked" (Luke 6:32–33, 35).

Throughout the Gospels, we read of instances in which God was moved by compassion: "When he saw the crowds, he had compassion on them" (Matthew 9:36); "Jesus called his disciples to him and said, 'I have compassion for these people'" (15:32); "Jesus said . . . 'Go and learn what this means: "I desire mercy [*hesed*], not sacrifice"'" (9:13). The word *hesed* in the Old Testament is translated as "God's loving kindness." Aren't you glad that you serve a God who is moved with compassion?

"God demonstrates his own love for us in this: While we were still sinners, Christ died for us" (Romans 5:8). That should be all the proof we need, yet many believers question God's love for them. God presupposed this when He inspired Paul to write, "I pray that you, being rooted and established in love, may have power, together with the Lord's holy people, to grasp how wide and long and high and deep is the love of Christ, and to know this love that surpasses knowledge—that you may be filled to the measure of all the fullness of God" (Ephesians 3:17–19).

Why do you think so many people question God's love for them?

_____

_____

_____

How has God demonstrated His love for us?

_____

_____

_____

How is God's love (*agape*) different from brotherly love (*phileo*)?

_____

_____

_____

What has caused you personally to question God's love for you? How can that be rectified?

_____

_____

_____

In what ways have you failed to love someone (to do what is right on his or her behalf) because you didn't like that person?

_____

_____

_____

According to strict truth, God is incomprehensible and incapable of being measured. For whatever the knowledge is that we are able to obtain about God—either by perception or by reflection—we must of necessity believe that He is far better by many degrees than what we perceive Him to be.

Origen (AD 184–253)

2

God Is Merciful and Good

Psalm 100:1–5

Key Point

God is the author of life, and in His mercy and goodness He makes right what His rebellious creation has made wrong.

Key Verse

For the Lord is good and his love endures forever.

Psalm 100:5

Jesus said, "There is only One who is good" (Matthew 19:17), and He, of course, is God. Therefore, everything God does is good, and we are the benefactors of His goodness. "And we know that in all things God works for the good of those who love him, who have been called according to his purpose" (Romans 8:28). However, our finite minds struggle to understand the infinite goodness of God.

First, we don't really know what is good for us. What tastes good often proves to be unhealthy. What looks good may be so in appearance only.

What feels good can lead us astray. Even a treacherous act, such as the one Joseph's brothers committed, can bring about a greater good. Joseph said to them, "You intended to harm me, but God intended it for good to accomplish what is now being done" (Genesis 50:20).

Still, when we read how God utterly destroyed the Amalekites (see 1 Samuel 15:2–3), it doesn't seem as if His actions are consistent with His goodness. However, that view is from our limited human perspective, which may be overlooking God's justice. If we know there is cancer in the body, the loving thing to do is cut it out. If there is a rotten apple in a barrel, the good thing to do is to get rid of it. We have a small role in the larger drama of life and only see a tiny portion of the big picture God is painting.

Second, we don't understand why—if God is all-powerful and good— bad things happen to good people. It is impossible to answer that question unless we understand that there are evil forces in this world that are actively opposing the will of God. God created Lucifer, the beautiful angel of light, to be a light bearer. Lucifer turned his back on God and became Satan, the deceiver and the accuser. God created Adam and Eve, and by their choice they lost their relationship with God, which made it possible for Satan to have dominion in this world.

Consequently, evil forces are at work in this world—forces that oppose the will of God. "Yet you say, 'The way of the Lord is not just.' Hear, you Israelites: Is my way unjust? Is it not your ways that are unjust?" (Ezekiel 18:25). "'Do I take any pleasure in the death of the wicked?' declares the Sovereign LORD. 'Rather, am I not pleased when they turn from their ways and live?'" (verse 23). God is the author of life, not death, and He is in the process of making right what His rebellious creation has made wrong. The goodness of God will overcome this present evil—if not in our lifetime, then surely in the future.

God is also merciful. "But when the kindness and love of God our Savior appeared, he saved us, not because of righteous things we had done, but because of his mercy" (Titus 3:4–5). To be merciful to others is to not give them what they deserve. We deserved hell, but God was merciful and gave us eternal life. David said, "Taste and see that the LORD is good" (Psalm 34:8) and "surely your goodness and love [mercy] will follow me all the days of my life, and I will dwell in the house of the LORD forever" (Psalm 23:6).

In what ways do our finite minds tend to struggle with the concept of God's goodness and mercy?

How can our human perspective fail to comprehend the nature of God's goodness and mercy?

How is God's goodness and mercy working through His children to make right what His rebellious creation has made wrong?

Count your blessings by listing all the good things God has done for you:

To be merciful means to not give others what they deserve. How has God demonstrated His mercy to you?

_____

_____

_____

When Paul says "all things" [Romans 8:28] he mentions even the things that seem painful. For if tribulation, or poverty, or imprisonment, or famines, or deaths or anything else should come upon us, God can change them into the opposite. For this is one instance of His ineffable power, that He can make painful things appear light to us and turn them into things that can be helpful. Paul talks about being called "according to His purpose" in order to show that the calling itself is not enough. . . . The calling was not forced on anyone, nor was it compulsory. Everyone was called, but not everyone obeyed the call. . . . Even opposition and disappointments are turned into good, which is exactly what happened to this remarkable man, the apostle Paul.

John Chrysostom (AD 347–407)

3

God Is Gracious and Kind

Hebrews 4:14–16

Key Point

God, being merciful, did not give us what we deserved, and He graciously took the next step and gave us what we didn't deserve.

Key Verse

Let us then approach God's throne of grace with confidence, so that we may receive mercy and find grace to help us in our time of need.

Hebrews 4:16

God is righteous and cannot be unjust at any time. To administer justice is to give people what they deserve. If justice were served, we would all have to face eternity in hell. But God is also merciful, and because of His love, He did not want to give us what we deserved. Instead, Jesus satisfied the righteous demands of God by paying the price for our sins. "But when the kindness and love of God our Savior appeared, he saved us, not because of righteous things we had done, but because of his mercy" (Titus 3:4–5).

Grace is like the flipside of mercy. Grace is giving people what they don't deserve. Because of God's mercy, He looked for another way to satisfy His justice so that we would not have to pay our own wages for sin, which is death. Because of His gracious nature, He gave us eternal life. "For it is by grace you have been saved, through faith—and this not from yourselves, it is the gift of God—not by works, so that no one can boast" (Ephesians 2:8–9). Grace is unwarranted favor. It cannot be purchased and it cannot be earned. We can only respond to a gracious gift by humbly receiving it, giving thanks, and then praising the character of the giver.

In order to bear the sins of humanity, Jesus "made himself nothing by taking the very nature of a servant, being made in human likeness" (Philippians 2:7). He became one of us in order to be our "kinsman redeemer." He became our scapegoat (substitute) by taking our place on the cross. There is another benefit of Jesus' becoming one of us: He can relate to us in every way. He faced every temptation, suffered every hardship, and was totally rejected. He spoke the truth and loved sacrificially. "For we do not have a high priest who is unable to empathize with our weaknesses, but we have one who has been tempted in every way, just as we are—yet he did not sin" (Hebrews 4:15).

Being omniscient, God fully understood the suffering and hardship of fallen humanity. He didn't have to become one of us in order to know and feel our plight. God already knew what we thought and how we felt, and His plans were in place long before Jesus came. The limitation is in our understanding, not His. It would be harder for us to believe that Jesus actually does "empathize with our weaknesses" if He had never suffered or been tempted as we are.

People don't want to share their burdens with someone they don't think can relate to them or understand their situation. Nor do people unburden themselves to those who are unable to help them. Jesus not only understands, but He also responds to us kindly, because He is kind and loving by nature. God gives us what we need, not what we deserve, because by nature He is gracious. He has called us to do the same to others: "Be merciful, just as your Father is merciful" (Luke 6:36). In other words, don't give to others what they deserve; but don't stop there. Give them what they don't deserve—that is, love one another.

What is the difference between justice, mercy, and grace?

For what two reasons did Jesus take on the form of humanity?

How can we know that God understands our suffering and hardships?

How does it help you to know that Jesus was tempted in every way and suffered to the point of death for your sake?

What will happen to you if you come boldly before the throne of grace? What will happen if you don't?

_____

_____

_____

How is it that we should "approach boldly"? Because now it is a throne of grace, not a throne of judgment. Therefore, boldly, "that we may obtain mercy," even such as we are seeking. For the affair is one of munificence [very generous]; a royal largess [liberal giving]. "And may find grace to help in time of need." He said well, "for help in time of need." If you approach now, He means, you will receive both grace and mercy, for you approach "in time of need." . . . Now He sits granting a pardon, but when the end comes, then He rises up to judgment.

John Chrysostom (AD 347–407)

4

God Is Faithful

Psalm 89:1–52

Key Point

Our confidence in God is rooted in His faithfulness.

Key Verses

But as surely as God is faithful . . . no matter how many promises God has made, they are "Yes" in Christ.

2 Corinthians 1:18, 20

It is hard to relate to people you can't trust or count on when needed, but you can count on God because He is eternally consistent and faithful. The psalmist says, "I will declare that your love stands firm forever, that you have established your faithfulness in heaven itself" (Psalm 89:2). The fact that God made the world and all that is in it, and that He demonstrates His faithfulness by providing for His creatures, is abundantly illustrated in the "nature psalms," such as Psalm 104. His faithful provision for His Chosen People is best seen in His plan for redemption as evidenced in His promises and covenants.

The Old Testament is a record of God's faithfulness in redeeming His people, from the call of Abraham to the establishment of the Israelites in the Promised Land. The Exodus from Egypt demonstrated God's faithfulness (see Exodus 15:1–17), and it caused those who had been delivered to believe in Yahweh and His servant Moses (see 14:31). For generations, even up to our own day, the Jewish people have commemorated the deliverance from Egypt and the Passover in remembrance of God's faithfulness.

From the time God made a covenant with Abraham in Genesis 12:1–3, His unlikely promises were slowly but progressively fulfilled even when they seemed to be humanly impossible and in spite of overwhelming odds. The Messianic line began with Sarah, who gave birth to Isaac when she no longer humanly could, and then God provided a scapegoat to take the place of Isaac when he was ordered to be sacrificed, preserving Abraham and Sarah's posterity. God promised that the seed of the woman would continue through the house of David and that the Messiah would sit on the throne of David. "Once for all, I have sworn by my holiness—and I will not lie to David—that his line will continue forever and his throne endure before me like the sun; it will be established forever like the moon, the faithful witness in the sky" (Psalm 89:35–37).

The first two chapters of Luke's gospel paint a vivid picture of people who were waiting expectantly for God to fulfill His promises made under the Old Covenant (see Luke 2:25–38). Simeon saw the fulfillment in the birth of Jesus and rejoiced in God's faithfulness: "Sovereign Lord, as you have promised, you may now dismiss your servant in peace. For my eyes have seen your salvation, which you have prepared in the sight of all people" (Luke 2:29–31).

From the days of Abraham, many people probably thought that God was unfaithful, and so they lost their faith in Him when His Word was not fulfilled in their lifetime. "But do not forget this one thing, dear friends: With the Lord a day is like a thousand years, and a thousand years are like a day. The Lord is not slow in keeping his promise, as some understand slowness" (2 Peter 3:8–9). There was a faithful remnant, however, who chose to believe in God in spite of incredible hardships and persecution (see Hebrews 11). "These were all commended for their faith, yet none of them received what had been promised, since God had planned something

better for us so that only together with us would they be made perfect"
(Hebrews 11:39–40).

How much is our confidence in God based on His keeping His word,
covenants, and promises?

_____

_____

_____

What evidence do we find in the Old Testament of God's faithfulness to
His Chosen People? Are Christians His Chosen People (see 1 Peter 2:9–10)?

_____

_____

_____

Why don't some people trust God if He is faithful? How might that relate
to God's timing?

_____

_____

_____

Have you ever lost your trust in God because you thought or heard that
He is unfaithful or that He had broken a promise? Explain.

_____

_____

_____

_____

How important is it to your faith to know that some covenants and promises are conditional ("if you will, then I will," which is dependent on you), as opposed to those that are unconditional ("I will," which is dependent on God)?

_____

_____

_____

Paul had to explain why he could not keep his promise [2 Corinthians 1:18], so that the Corinthians would not distrust his preaching. In fact what Paul was preaching was reliable. His promise to come to them had been from himself, but the message he proclaimed was from God, and God cannot lie.

John Chrysostom (AD 347–407)

5

God Is Immutable

Numbers 23:13–20

Key Point

The changeless nature of God is what makes Him the ultimate object of our faith.

Key Verse

God is not human, that he should lie, not a human being, that he should change his mind. Does he speak and then not act? Does he promise and not fulfill?

Numbers 23:19

"The grass withers and the flowers fall, but the word of our God endures forever" (Isaiah 40:8). The Word and character of God never change, which is in stark contrast to that of humanity, which is in a constant state of change. The changeless nature of God is what makes Him the ultimate object of our faith. The writer of Hebrews says, "Remember your leaders, who spoke the word of God to you. Consider the outcome of their way of life and imitate their faith. Jesus Christ is the same yesterday and today and forever" (Hebrews 13:7–8).

Note that the writer doesn't say we should necessarily imitate the behavior of those who lead us. Our faith is not based on humanity, no matter how well people behave. We should consider the lives of teachers who profess to know God and live by faith, and then imitate what they believe if their lives are bearing the fruit of righteousness. When we see the fruit of righteousness in the lives of our leaders, we know that the object of their faith is God and His Word, which never change.

Fallen humanity has "worshiped and served created things rather than the Creator" (Romans 1:25). Many believers have been led astray by trusting only in themselves or others, because there are no perfectly faithful people. We are not able to solve our own problems, much less save ourselves. Humanity has found some stability by trusting in the fixed order of the universe, especially the solar system. We set our watches by it and plan our calendars.

What would happen tomorrow if the sun rose two hours later than it was supposed to rise? The whole world would be thrown into chaos, and everyone would be extremely anxious. It takes months or years for us to establish faith in someone or something. One act of unfaithfulness or inconsistency can destroy that trust, and it will take months or years of consistent, faithful behavior to rebuild it. In fact, we would be foolish to put our trust in someone or something that is unfaithful or unreliable. That is one reason why human relationships are so fragile.

This is not the case concerning our relationship with God. God is faithful and never changes, and understanding this provides stability in our lives. We can confidently live by faith in God, knowing that the Creator who sustains the fixed order of the universe will also sustain us. The psalmist declares, "In the beginning you laid the foundations of the earth, and the heavens are the work of your hands. They will perish, but you remain; they will all wear out like a garment. Like clothing you will change them and they will be discarded. But you remain the same, and your years will never end" (Psalm 102:25–27).

"What if some were unfaithful? Will their unfaithfulness nullify God's faithfulness? Not at all! Let God be true, and every human being a liar" (Romans 3:3–4). God's Word is true whether we believe it or not, and He will never change. He keeps His Word and His Covenant, being faithful to Himself. He is the rock of our salvation, who changes not.

Why does God's unchanging nature allow us to completely put our faith in Him?

Why may it be foolish to put our trust in others or the things of this world?

Does our unfaithfulness have any impact on His faithfulness? Why or why not?

How does it affect your confidence and stability to know that God will never change?

What relationships in your past or present have been broken because others have changed in such a way that they were no longer believable?

The natural properties of the Word who came forth from the Father were maintained even when He became flesh. It is foolish therefore to dare to introduce a breach. For the Lord Jesus Christ is one and through Him the Father created all things. He is composed of human properties and of others that are above the human, yielding a kind of middle term. He is, in fact, a mediator between God and humankind, according to the Scriptures, God by nature even when incarnate, truly, not purely man like us, remaining what He was even when He had become flesh. For it is written, "Jesus Christ is the same yesterday, and today and forever."

Cyril of Alexandria (AD 376–444)

Levels of Prayer

Psalm 95 is a model for approaching God in prayer. It begins with praise and thanksgiving: "Let us come before him *with thanksgiving*" (Psalm 95:2, emphasis added). In the New Testament, the apostle Paul seldom mentioned prayer without an attitude of gratitude: "I have not stopped *giving thanks* for you, remembering you in my prayers" (Ephesians 1:16, emphasis added); "Do not be anxious about anything, but in every situation, by prayer and petition, *with thanksgiving*, present your requests to God" (Philippians 4:6); "Devote yourselves to prayer, being watchful and *thankful*" (Colossians 4:2, emphasis added); "Rejoice always; pray continuously; *give thanks* in all circumstances" (1 Thessalonians 5:16–18, emphasis added).

There are three levels of communicating with God in prayer. Each level incorporates praise and thanksgiving. The first level is petition, which Paul mentioned in Philippians 4:6. James adds, "You do not have because you do not ask God" (4:2). However, he qualifies this by saying, "When you ask, you do not receive, because you ask with wrong motives, that you may spend what you get on your pleasures" (verse 3). As discussed previously, petitions should be consistent with the Lord's Prayer.

Petition is all too often one-way communication. People tire of that, but the next level of prayer is personal and more like a dialogue. In Psalm 95:7–8, the psalmist says that as you personally and humbly approach God and "hear his voice, do not harden your hearts." The word "hear" means to listen so as to obey. If you heard from God, you may be inclined to "harden your hearts," since the first items on God's list are issues that concern your relationship with Him. So, if there are unresolved moral issues that you have never confessed to God, rest assured that they will be at the top of His list.

All those distracting thoughts that we struggled with while petitioning Him in level one are from God or allowed by God to get our attention, even if they are from the enemy. The Lord wants us to actively deal with whatever comes to our minds during prayer. There is nothing we can't talk to God about, because He already knows the thoughts and attitudes of our hearts (see Hebrews 4:12–13). These issues are critical because they relate to our relationship with God, which is always His first concern.

When prayer becomes this personal, we begin to pray continually (see 1 Thessalonians 5:17). This makes intercessory prayer possible, which is the highest level. There are few true intercessors who are intimate enough with God to hear His voice and obey. Intercessors hear from God, sense the burden to pray, and continue in prayer until the burden leaves. Seldom, if ever, is their prayer time in public. It is usually in the privacy of their homes and often late at night. God accomplishes much of His work through these dear saints who know how to pray.

A New Understanding of God's Nature

Defining the Trinity and the deity of Christ are the two most critical doctrines of the Church, and it was the primary concern for the Church's ecumenical councils during its first 500 years. The early Church leaders didn't completely formulate how full deity and full humanity could be combined together in one person until the council of Chalcedon in 451, when they adopted the Chalcedonian Definition. By that time the Church refuted the following doctrines as heresies:

Sabellianism: Sabellius (c. AD 215) taught that the Father and the Son and the Holy Spirit were one person who appeared to people in three different forms or modes. This idea, also known as "modalism," denies the personal relationship within the Trinity that is mentioned a number of times in Scripture.

Arianism: Arius (AD 250–336) denied the full deity of Christ and the Holy Spirit. Variations of this heresy are taught today by the Mormons and Jehovah's Witnesses.

Apollinarianism: Apollinaris of Laodicea (d. AD 390) taught that Jesus had a human body but not a human mind or spirit. Christ had to be fully and truly human if He was to save us (see Hebrews 2:17).

Nestorianism: Nestorius (AD 386–450) taught there were two separate persons in Christ—a human person and a divine person.

Monophysitism: This was an idea proposed by Eutyches (AD 380–456), who taught that Christ had only one nature.

Daily Readings

1. The Trinity	Acts 2:32–36
2. I Am Who I Am	Exodus 3:1–15
3. The Last Adam	1 Corinthians 15:45–54
4. The Deity of Christ	Philippians 2:1–11
5. The Holy Spirit	Acts 1:2–11

1

The Trinity

Acts 2:32–36

Key Point

The Bible teaches that there is one God who exists in three persons: the Father, the Son, and the Holy Spirit.

Key Verse

Therefore go and make disciples of all nations, baptizing them in the name of the Father and of the Son and of the Holy Spirit.

Matthew 28:19

Hear O Israel: The LORD our God, the LORD is one" (Deuteronomy 6:4). Old Testament Judaism and New Testament Christianity both stress monotheism (one God) as opposed to polytheism (many gods), pantheism (all is God), or atheism (no god or gods). Only Christianity recognizes the divine three-in-oneness—the eternal coexistence of the Father, Son, and Holy Spirit in the inner personal life of the Godhead.

The plural nature of the Godhead is revealed in the first chapter of Genesis through the use of the plural pronoun: "Then God said, 'Let us make mankind in our image, in our likeness'" (1:26). Jesus explicitly revealed the doctrine of the Trinity in the baptismal formula: "Therefore go and make disciples of all nations, baptizing them in the name of the Father and of the Son and of the Holy Spirit" (Matthew 28:19). The Epistles are saturated with the revelation of the triune Godhead, uniting all three as the agents of our salvation and sanctification: "You, however, are not in the realm of the flesh but are in the realm of the Spirit, if indeed the Spirit of God lives in you. And if anyone does not have the Spirit of Christ, they do not belong to Christ" (Romans 8:9).

Although the Father, Son, and Holy Spirit work in unity, everything flows from the Father. Jesus said He could do nothing on His own initiative (see John 5:30; 8:42) and modeled a life that was totally dependent on the Father (see John 17:7). In this way, He left us an example that we ought to follow in His steps (see 1 Peter 2:21), for we too are called to live dependently on God. Likewise, the Holy Spirit comes from the Father (see John 15:26), and He will not speak on His own (see John 16:13). As we approach the Father, we do so in the name of the Lord Jesus Christ as led by the Holy Spirit. The sacrificial death and the resurrection of Jesus Christ are the only basis by which we can approach our heavenly Father, and it is the unique work of the Holy Spirit to bear witness with our spirit that we are children of God (see Romans 8:16) and to lead us into all truth (see John 16:13).

After Pentecost, Peter's message brought together the finished work of Christ and the outpouring of the Holy Spirit. The coming of the Holy Spirit was the evidence that Jesus has been exalted to the right hand of the heavenly Father. During the three-year public ministry of Jesus, "the Spirit had not been given, since Jesus had not yet been glorified" (John 7:39). "Therefore let all Israel be assured of this: God has made this Jesus, whom you crucified, both Lord [*kurios*] and Messiah" (Acts 2:36). *Kurios* (Lord) is used to refer to Jesus in Jude 1:4 and is used to refer to God the Father in Jude 1:5.

The Athanasian Creed, which was formulated by the Early Church, affirmed the triune nature of God: "We worship one God in Trinity, and Trinity in Unity, neither confounding the Persons, nor dividing the substance, for there is one Person of the Father, another of the Son, and another of the Holy Ghost; but the godhead of the Father, of the Son and of the Holy Ghost is one, the glory equal, the majesty co-eternal."

What evidence do we have from the Bible that God exists as three persons—Father, Son, and Holy Spirit?

Why is it so important that we believe that Jesus is fully God and was fully man?

How did the outpouring of the Holy Spirit on the Day of Pentecost reveal that Jesus had been "exalted to the right hand of God"?

To whom are you praying when you pray to God? How does prayer involve the Trinity?

Who are you serving when you serve God? How does serving God employ the Trinity?

_____

_____

_____

We . . . believe that there is only one God, but under the following dispensation or "economy," as it is called. We believe that this one only God has also a Son, His Word, who proceeded from Himself, by whom all things were made, and without whom nothing was made. Him we believe to have been sent by the Father into the virgin, and to have been born of her—being both man and God, the son of man and the Son of God. . . . And the Son also sent from heaven from the Father, according to His own promise, the Holy Spirit, the Paraclete, the sanctifier of the faith of those who believe in the Father, the Son, and the Holy Spirit.

Tertullian (AD 160–220)

2

I Am Who I Am

Exodus 3:1–15

Key Point

God revealed Himself as the great "I am," meaning that what He was in the past is who He is in the present and will be in the future.

Key Verse

I told you that you would die in your sins; if you do not believe that I am he, you will indeed die in your sins.

John 8:24

God called Moses to deliver the Israelites out of bondage in Egypt and lead them to the Promised Land. When Moses asked how he was going to tell the people that God had sent him, the Lord responded by saying, "I am who I am. This is what you are to say to the Israelites: 'I am has sent me to you'" (Exodus 3:14). God also said, "Say to the Israelites, 'The Lord, the God of your fathers—the God of Abraham, the God of Isaac and the God of Jacob—has sent me to you.' This is my name forever, the name you shall call me from generation to generation" (verse 15).

The name "I AM" means that what God was in the past He is in the present and will be in the future. The most distinctive name the Israelites had for God was Yahweh (Jehovah), which comes from the same root as "I AM." This name was given to Moses to convince the children of Israel that God was faithful to His covenant and that He would lead them out of bondage. The name does not disclose who He is in Himself; rather, it discloses who He is, was, and will be in relationship to the people of God.

The name is mentioned in the New Testament when Jesus responded to the Jews, "Very truly I tell you . . . before Abraham was born, *I am!*" (John 8:58, emphasis added). Whereas Moses was the lawgiver who led God's people from slavery in Egypt to the Promised Land, Jesus fulfilled the Law and led God's people from slavery to sin to freedom in Christ and eternal life. The God of Abraham, Isaac, and Jacob is the same God who delivers us from the kingdom of darkness to the kingdom of His beloved Son (see Colossians 1:13). Jesus said, "Unless you believe that *I AM* who I claim to be, you will die in your sins" (John 8:24 NLT, emphasis added).

John records a number of other "I am" statements made by Jesus. To the crowds He said, "*I am* the bread of life" (John 6:48, emphasis added). Like the manna from heaven that sustained the physical life of the Israelites, Jesus also came from heaven to give us spiritual life. To Mary and Martha, He said, "*I am* the resurrection and the life. The one who believes in me will live, even though they die; and whoever lives by believing in me will never die" (John 11:25–26, emphasis added). In other words, if we believe in Jesus, we will continue to live spiritually even when we die physically.

On other occasions, Jesus said, "I tell you the truth, *I am* the gate for the sheep" (John 10:7, emphasis added), and "*I am* the way and the truth and the life. No one comes to the Father except through me" (John 14:6, emphasis added). Finally, Jesus said, "*I am* the good shepherd. The good shepherd lays down his life for the sheep" (John 10:11, emphasis added). "We are his people, the sheep of his pasture" (Psalm 100:3). "Salvation is found in no one else, for there is no other name under heaven given to mankind by which we must be saved" (Acts 4:12).

What does the name "I AM" imply?

What kinds of similar statements did Jesus make about His nature? How do these statements show that He and the Father are one?

What does the statement "unless you believe that I am He, you shall die in your sins" say about cults and salvation?

How does knowing that "I AM" is an all-encompassing concept (time and space) affect you personally?

How should you live knowing that your soul is in union with I AM?

_____

_____

_____

Analyze the idea of mutability and you will find was and will be: contemplate God, and you will find the is where was and will be cannot exist. . . . And so, by these words, "If you do not believe that I am," I think our Lord meant nothing else than this, "If you do not believe that I am" God, "you shall die in your sins." Well, God be thanked that He said, "If you do not believe" and did not say: If you do not comprehend. For who can comprehend this?

Augustine of Hippo (AD 354–430)

3

The Last Adam

1 Corinthians 15:45–54

Key Point

Jesus not only came to give us life; He is our life.

Key Verse

In him was life, and that life was the light of all mankind.

John 1:4

T he first Adam was born both physically and spiritually alive. Because Adam sinned, he died spiritually and was separated from God. Physical death was also a consequence of sin, although Adam did not physically die until many years after the Fall. From that time on, every descendant of Adam and Eve has been born physically alive but spiritually dead (see Ephesians 2:1).

Yet God had a plan for restoring life and giving His people a new identity and position in Christ. He promised that redemption would come through the seed of a woman (see Genesis 3:15; 17:19; Galatians 3:16). As the years passed, the Israelites became impatient and wondered how they would know the Messiah when He finally did come. "Therefore the Lord himself will give you a sign: The virgin will conceive and give birth to a son, and will call him Immanuel" (Isaiah 7:14).

The last book of the Old Testament was written 400 years before "the Word became flesh and made his dwelling among us" (John 1:14). The prophecy was fulfilled concerning Immanuel, which means "God is with us," and the Virgin Mary was greatly amazed (see Luke 1:34–35).

Nobody can fully explain the mystery of the Incarnation, but Scripture clearly teaches that the eternal Son became flesh. So critical is the doctrine of the Incarnation that Scripture makes it a primary test of orthodoxy (core Christian doctrine): "This is how you can recognize the Spirit of God: Every spirit that acknowledges that Jesus Christ has come in the flesh is from God, but every spirit that does not acknowledge Jesus is not from God. This is the spirit of the antichrist, which you have heard is coming and even now is already in the world" (1 John 4:2–3).

The Incarnation is what sets Christianity apart from the cults and all the other religions of the world. They may believe in the historical Jesus, but they do not believe that God became man. They believe that God could appear as a man—like an apparition—and suffer in appearance only, but unless they have the Holy Spirit they will not say that Jesus was fully God while also fully human.

This union between divinity and humanity was necessary in order to bring us spiritual life. "In him was life, and that life was the light of all mankind" (John 1:4). Notice that light does not produce life. The light of believers is the radiation of the eternal life of God. The last Adam—Jesus—like the first Adam, was also born physically and spiritually alive. But unlike the first Adam, Jesus never sinned, even though He was tempted in every way (see Hebrews 4:15).

The virgin birth was necessary because Jesus came to give us life. Jesus said, "I have come that they may have life, and have it to the full" (John 10:10). What Adam and Eve lost in the Fall was eternal life, and that is what Jesus came to restore. He did not come to give us a more fulfilling physical life with material blessings. Rather, He came to give us a fulfilling spiritual life filled with spiritual blessings, which are love, joy, peace, patience, kindness, goodness, faithfulness, gentleness, and self-control—the fruit of the Spirit (see Galatians 5:22–23). Jesus didn't just come to give us life. He is our life (see Colossians 3:4).

Review 1 Corinthians 15:45–54. What does Paul mean when he says that the first Adam became a "living being" but the last Adam a "life-giving spirit"?

_____

_____

_____

Why is the virgin birth so critical to Christian doctrine?

_____

_____

_____

How does the Incarnation of Christ set Christianity apart from other religions? Why is it critical for us that Jesus was human while also divine?

_____

_____

_____

Can you defend from Scripture the orthodox teaching that Christ had two natures (fully God and fully man), while being one person (no split personality)? Explain.

_____

_____

_____

How is Jesus your life?

_____

_____

_____

Christ could not be described as being man without flesh, nor the Son of man without any human parent. Just as He is not God without the Spirit of God, nor the Son of God without having God for His Father. Thus the origin of the two substances displayed Him as man and God. In one respect, He was born; in the other respect, He was unborn. In one respect, fleshly; in the other, spiritual. In one sense, weak; in the other, exceedingly strong. In one sense, dying; in the other sense, living. This property of the two states—the divine and the human—is distinctly asserted with equal truth of both natures alike.

Tertullian (AD 160–220)

4

The Deity of Christ

Philippians 2:1–11

Key Point

Jesus voluntarily surrendered use of His divine attributes to become like us.

Key Verse

He made himself nothing by taking the very nature of a servant, being made in human likeness.

Philippians 2:7

Jesus' claim that He was the promised Messiah and the eternal Son of God infuriated the Jewish leaders (see John 5:18) and caused them to accuse Jesus of blasphemy (see John 10:33). Paul was part of that crowd, but he would later write that Jesus was "in very nature [*morphe*] God" (Philippians 2:6), and in His Incarnation, He embraced perfect humanity.

The key word is *morphe*, which is translated as "nature" or "form." The word stresses the inner essence or reality of that with which it is associated. Jesus "did not consider equality with God something to be grasped" (verse 6). In other words, Jesus did not have to strive to be God or even be like Him, because He was and is God. He voluntarily surrendered independent use of His own divine attributes. When the devil tempted Jesus to turn the rocks into bread, He simply responded, "Man shall not live on bread alone, but on every word that comes from the mouth of God" (Matthew 4:4). The devil wanted Jesus to use His own divine attributes independently of the Father to save Himself. He could have called on 10,000 angels to save Him from death on the cross.

Jesus "made himself nothing by taking the very nature [*morphe*] of a servant, being made in human likeness" (Philippians 2:7). "Made himself nothing" literally means "He emptied Himself." He divested Himself of His self-interest, but not of His deity. Jesus humbled Himself and took on the very nature of man. He was truly God and also truly man. "Likeness" means similar but different. He differed from the rest of humanity in that He was sinless. His self-renunciation was necessary if He was to have an authentic human experience that included geographical limitations, human development in mind and body, and the need for food and sleep. He had to totally depend on the heavenly Father.

The phrase "being found in appearance as a man" (verse 8) refers to a temporary and outer appearance in contrast to *morphe*, which signifies a permanent inner quality. The condescension of Jesus included not only His birth but also His death, which was the worst possible "death—even death on a cross!" (verse 8). Martin Luther said, "The mystery of the humanity of Christ, that he sunk Himself into our flesh, is beyond all human understanding." Jesus left His exalted position to be like us in order to die for us. To a similar but far lesser degree, we are called to humble ourselves under God's mighty hand so that He might lift us up in due time (see 1 Peter 5:6).

For us to become a worm to save a worm doesn't remotely compare to Almighty God becoming a man to save humanity. Jesus' life was the epitome of humble submission leading to an excruciating physical death. On the cross, "Jesus called out with a loud voice, 'Father, into your hands I commit my spirit.' When he had said this, he breathed his last" (Luke 23:46). His physical life ended, because His body was no longer in union with His Spirit, but He will forever remain our life, which is safely in the hands of God.

How do you explain the complete reversal of Paul from being a persecutor of the Church to its ardent defender? Was it a philosophical shift or a change of life?

What is significant about the word *morphe* as it relates to Christ?

Why did Jesus refuse to use His divine attributes to save Himself when Satan tempted Him in the wilderness?

How does the Incarnation speak directly to our pride?

How does the example of Jesus emptying Himself speak directly to our need to submit to God and serve others?

_____

_____

_____

If we take Him simply and solely to be a man made from a woman, how could He be said to be in the form equal to the Father? If only a man, how could He have the fullness that would make sense of His being emptied? What height could He have occupied before that He might be said to have "humbled Himself"? How did He "come to be in the likeness of men" if He was already so by nature?

Cyril of Alexandria (AD 376–444)

5

The Holy Spirit

Acts 1:2–11

Key Point

The Holy Spirit communicates God's presence to us and enables us to live a righteous life.

Key Verse

Those who are led by the Spirit of God are the children of God.

Romans 8:14

John baptized believers with water, but he said that one greater than he would baptize with the Holy Spirit (see Matthew 3:11). The coming of the Holy Spirit, which was prophesied by Joel, happened at Pentecost (see Joel 2:28–32; Acts 2:17–21). "Up to that time the Spirit had not been given, since Jesus had not yet been glorified" (John 7:39). The promised coming of the Holy Spirit happened when Jesus was exalted at the right hand of the Father (see Acts 2:33).

The resurrected Jesus appeared to many of His followers during the course of 40 days and instructed them, "Do not leave Jerusalem, but wait for the gift my Father promised. . . . You will receive power when the Holy Spirit comes on you; and you will be my witnesses in Jerusalem, and in all Judea and Samaria, and to the ends of the earth" (Acts 1:4, 8). The Church Age began the moment believers received the Holy Spirit. Even though they had seen the resurrected Christ, they could not be witnesses until the resurrected life of Christ came to dwell within them through the power of the Holy Spirit. At Pentecost, they were filled and empowered by the Holy Spirit.

The Holy Spirit is not a cosmic force—He is the third person of the Trinity. God's Holy Spirit had inspired the Old Testament prophets, moved among His people, and been present with them in the person of Christ, but now He would dwell within us as the Spirit of Christ. The Church, or the Body of Christ, is comprised of those believers who are born again spiritually by the action of the Holy Spirit. The Holy Spirit bears witness with their spirit that they are children of God (see Romans 8:16). Every believer, upon the simple condition of faith in Christ, is reborn (or regenerated, see Titus 3:5); baptized by the Holy Spirit into the Body of Christ (see 1 Corinthians 12:13); indwelt perpetually (see Romans 8:38–39); sealed (see Ephesians 1:13–14); and given the privilege of being filled by the Holy Spirit continuously (see Ephesians 5:18).

Jesus promised, "I will ask the Father, and he will give you another advocate to help you and be with you forever—the Spirit of truth" (John 14:16–17). The Holy Spirit is first and foremost the Spirit of truth, and "he will guide you into all truth" (John 16:13), and that truth will set you free (see John 8:32). Jesus said, "He will glorify me because it is from me that he will receive what he will make known to you" (John 16:14). The primary work of the Holy Spirit is to communicate God's presence to us, and because of the indwelling Holy Spirit, we have the power to live a righteous life. "For those who are led by the Spirit of God are the children of God" (Romans 8:14).

The Early Church was persecuted for their belief in God and discovered their need to maintain an intimate relationship with Him. They had been baptized into Christ, and now they needed to be continuously filled with the Spirit. "After they prayed, the place where they were meeting was shaken. And they were all filled with the Holy Spirit and spoke the word of God boldly" (Acts 4:31).

What did the coming of the Holy Spirit enable the early followers of Christ to do?

_____

_____

_____

In the Old Testament, the Holy Spirit inspired the prophets and moved among God's people. What role would He now play after the Day of Pentecost?

_____

_____

_____

What evidence in Scripture reveals that the Holy Spirit is the third member of the Trinity?

_____

_____

_____

How does the Holy Spirit enable you to be all that God created you to be?

_____

_____

_____

Why is it necessary for you to be continually filled with the Holy Spirit?

_____

_____

_____

_____

> *For with Him were always present the Word and Wisdom, the Son and the Spirit, by whom and in whom, freely and spontaneously, He made all things. This is to whom also He speaks, saying, "Let us make man after our image and likeness." . . . I have also largely demonstrated that the Word, namely the Son, was always with the Father. And that Wisdom also, who is the Spirit, was present with Him before all creation. He declares this by Solomon: "By Wisdom, God founded the earth, and understanding He has established the heavens." . . . There is therefore one God, who by the Word and Wisdom created and arranged all things.*
>
> Irenaeus (AD 130–202)

Praying by the Spirit

Jude, after warning about false teachers and the ungodliness of the last days, wrote, "But you, dear friends, [build] yourselves up in your most holy faith and [pray] in the Holy Spirit" (Jude 1:20). Paul also exhorts us to "pray in the Spirit on all occasions with all kinds of prayers and requests" (Ephesians 6:18).

We can only pray effectively as the Holy Spirit enables us, and we can only pray in the name of our Lord and Savior Jesus Christ. That does not mean we simply end a prayer by saying, "In Jesus' name, I pray"; it means we pray in a way that is consistent with the nature and purpose of Jesus. "In him and through faith in him we may approach God with freedom and confidence" (Ephesians 3:12).

If we are going to pray in the Spirit, we first need to be filled with the Spirit (see Ephesians 5:19–20). Then the Holy Spirit will enable us to pray, as Paul explains in Romans 8:26: "In the same way, the Spirit helps us in our weakness. We do not know what we ought to pray for, but the Spirit himself intercedes for us through wordless groans."

The word "helps" in the Greek is *sunantilambano*. It consists of two prepositions (*sun* and *anti*) before the verb *lambano*, which means "to take." Paul is saying that the Holy Spirit comes alongside us, bears us up, and takes us across to the other side (to God). The fact that we really don't know how or what to pray for demonstrates our weakness. The prayer that the Holy Spirit prompts us to pray is the prayer that God the Father will always answer. He leads us to pray as He guides our thoughts. His guidance may be so deep that words cannot express what we sense in our hearts. The Holy Spirit knows our hearts and knows the will of God.

The Holy Spirit not only helps us to pray, but also actually intercedes on our behalf. In fact, two members of the Trinity are continuously praying on our behalf. John says, "My dear children, I write this to you so that you will not sin. But if anybody does sin, we have an advocate with the Father—Jesus Christ, the Righteous One" (1 John 2:1). According to Paul, "Christ Jesus who died—more than that, who was raised to life—is at the right hand of God and is also interceding for us" (Romans 8:34). We have more help than we could ever comprehend.

As we walk with God, the Holy Spirit enables us to "pray without ceasing" (1 Thessalonians 5:17 NASB). Start by asking God to fill you with His Holy Spirit and thank Him for all that He is and for all that He has done for you. Then let the Holy Spirit disclose to your mind the will of your heavenly Father. He knows what to pray for, and He will continue to lead you throughout your day as you practice the presence of God.

A New Relationship
With God

A newly adopted child found himself in a big mansion. His new Father said, "This is your home, and you have a right to be here. I have made you a joint heir with my only begotten Son. He paid the price that set you free from your old taskmaster, who was cruel and condemning. I purchased it for you, because I love you."

The young boy couldn't help but question this incredible gift. This seems too good to be true, he thought. What did I do to deserve this? I have been a slave all my life, and I have done nothing to earn such a privilege!

He was deeply grateful, however, and soon began to explore all the rooms in the mansion. He formed new relationships with his adopted brothers and sisters and especially enjoyed the buffet table from which he freely ate. Then it happened! As he was turning away from the buffet table, he knocked over a valuable pitcher, which crashed to the floor and broke.

You clumsy, stupid kid! he thought. *You will never get away with this. What right do you have to be here? You better hide before someone finds out, because they will surely throw you out.* He was filled with guilt and shame. *Who do you think you are? Some kind of privileged person? The old taskmaster was right about me. I don't belong here. I belong in the basement!* So he descended into the cellar.

The basement was dreary, dark, and despairing. The only light came from the open door at the top of the long stairs from which he came. He heard his Father calling for him, but he was too ashamed to answer. He was surprised to find others there as well. Upstairs everybody talked to each other and joined in with daily projects that were fun and meaningful, but nobody talked to each other in the basement. They were too ashamed, and most felt that the cellar was where they really belonged anyway.

Old friends would occasionally come to the door and encourage them to come back upstairs. Not everybody stayed in the basement for the same reason. Some thought, *I deserve to be here. I was given a chance, but I blew it.* Others always had a reason why they couldn't return to their Father upstairs. Some were afraid they wouldn't be accepted.

The boy stayed in the basement, and the memory of what it was like to live upstairs begin to fade. So did his hope of ever returning. He questioned the love of this new Father and began to question whether he had ever been adopted in the first place. The noise of people having fun upstairs irritated him. The light upstairs had been warm and inviting, but now it was penetrating and revealing.

Then one day, a shaft of light penetrated his mind and reason returned. He began to think, *Why not throw myself on the mercy of this person who calls Himself my Father? What do I have to lose? Even if He makes me eat the crumbs that fall from the table, it would be better than this.* So the boy took the risk of climbing those stairs and facing his Father with the truth of what he had done.

"Lord," he said, "I knocked over some glasses and broke a pitcher." Without saying a word, his Father took him by the hand and led him into the dining room. To his utter amazement, his Father had prepared a banquet for him. "Welcome home, son," his Father said. "There is now no condemnation for those who are in Christ Jesus" (Romans 8:1).

Daily Readings

1. Adopted	Galatians 4:1–7
2. A Right Standing	Jeremiah 52:31–34
3. Peace With God	Judges 6:1–24
4. Access to God	Hebrews 10:19–25
5. The Coming of the Holy Spirit	Joel 2:28–32

1

Adopted
Galatians 4:1–7

Key Point

It is not by means of an accidental birth that we have been adopted as sons and daughters into the family of God.

Key Verses

In love he predestined us for adoption to sonship through Jesus Christ, in accordance with his pleasure and will.

Ephesians 1:4–5

The Thirteenth Amendment officially abolished slavery in the United States on December 18, 1865. So, how many slaves were there on December 19, 1865? In reality, none, but many people still lived like slaves. Some did so because they had never learned the truth that they were indeed free. Some didn't believe the truth and continued to live as they had been taught. Others reasoned that they were still doing the same thing that slaves did, so they must still be slaves. They maintained their slave identity because of the things they did.

One former slave, however, heard the good news and received it with great joy. He checked out the validity of the amendment and discovered that the highest of all authorities had originated the decree, and that it personally cost that authority a tremendous price. As a result, the slave's life was transformed. He correctly reasoned that it would be hypocritical to believe that he was still a slave rather than believe the truth that he was free. He determined to live by what he knew to be true, and his experiences began to change rather dramatically. He realized that his old taskmaster had no authority over him and did not need to be obeyed. He gladly served the one who had set him free.

In Galatians 4:1–7, Paul says that we were all like little children (*nepios,* "child," in verse 1, in contrast with *huios,* "son," in verse 7) who were subservient to our guardians and trustees—similar to the way slaves are under the authority of their masters. Even though we had a birthright, we could not become heirs until the time appointed by our Father. "But when the set time had fully come, God sent his Son, born of a woman, born under the law, to redeem those under the law, that we might receive adoption to sonship" (verses 4–5). We were enslaved to the "elemental spiritual forces of the world" (verse 3) until Christ came and set us free. We were in bondage to the Mosaic Law or other religious systems.

Christ did two things for those who were under the yoke of slavery (see Galatians 5:1). First, He redeemed those under the Law. The Jews were enslaved to the whole Mosaic system; it was the bondage of legalism. Second, the Incarnation, death, and resurrection of Christ secured for all believers their birthright as adopted sons and daughters. "Because you are sons, God has sent forth the Spirit of His Son into your hearts, crying out, '*Abba,* Father!' Therefore you are no longer a slave but a son, and if a son, then an heir of God through Christ" (Galatians 4:6–7 NKJV). As believers we may not *feel* free from sin and we may not *feel* like children of God, but in reality we are. Our position in Christ is real truth, and we must choose to believe it.

The Holy Spirit resides in our hearts, ensuring our position in God's family. The Spirit moves us to pray, "*Abba,* Father." The word *Abba* is the Aramaic word for "father." Small children used it to address their father—it would be similar to the English word "daddy." Calling God "*Abba*" implies intimacy and trust as opposed to slavery and legalism.

If Christians have been liberated in Christ, why do you think so many still live as they always have?

What does it mean to be "in slavery under the elemental spiritual forces of the world"? To what or whom are they in bondage?

What are the positives of being adopted into the family of God?

As an adopted child, do you view God as a legalistic taskmaster or as a loving "Daddy"? Explain.

From what has God set you free?

_____

_____

_____

"The fullness of time" is the completed time which had been foreordained by God the Father for the sending of His Son, so that, made from a virgin, He might be born like a man, subjecting himself to the law up to His baptism, so that He might provide a way by which sinners, washed and snatched away from the yoke of the law, might be adopted as God's sons by His condescension, as He had promised to those redeemed by the blood of His Son. It was necessary, indeed, that the Savior should be made subject to the law, as a son of Abraham according to the flesh, so that, having been circumcised, He could be seen as the one promised to Abraham, who had come to justify the Gentiles through faith, since He bore the sign of the one to whom the promise had been made.

Ambrosiaster (written c. AD 366–384)

2

A Right Standing

Jeremiah 52:31–34

Key Point

By the grace of God we can stand before His throne with our relationship restored.

Key Verse

God raised us up with Christ and seated us with him in the heavenly realms in Christ Jesus.

Ephesians 2:6

After the fall of Jerusalem, Jehoiachin, the king of Judah, was exiled to Babylon and imprisoned. At the time, the king of the Babylonian empire was Awel-Marduk, the son of Nebuchadnezzar. (The name Awel-Marduk actually means the son or servant of the god Murduk.) Out of kindness, Awel-Marduk set Jehoiachin free, placed him in a position of honor, fellowshipped with him daily, and provided for all his needs.

This kingly act of grace is an Old Testament type (or foreshadowing) of what has been perfectly fulfilled in Christ. Israel had a covenant relationship with God, which was conditional. Had the people trusted God and been obedient, they would have enjoyed prosperity in the Promised Land. The Lord had said to His Covenant People, "Maintain justice and do what is right, for my salvation is close at hand and my righteousness will soon be revealed. Blessed is the one who does this—the person who holds it fast, who keeps the Sabbath without desecrating it, and keeps their hands from doing any evil" (Isaiah 56:1–2).

But the Chosen People were unable to keep the Law. The nation divided into Israel and Judah, and because of their disobedience, God raised up Assyria to defeat Israel in 722 BC. Finally, Judah fell along with Jerusalem in 586 BC. Because of Adam's sin, they had no legal relationship with God, causing them to stand guilty and under condemnation. Sin had severed their personal, moral relationship with Him, causing their nature to be impure and at odds with God's holiness.

	Pre-Fall Man	Post-Fall Man
Natural	Righteous	"By nature deserving of wrath" (Eph. 2:3)
Rational	Truthful and right	"Darkened in their understanding" (Eph. 4:18)
Spiritual	Alive	"Separated from the life of God" (Eph. 4:18)
Emotional	Safe, secure, free	"Having lost all sensitivity" (Eph. 4:19)
Volitional	Free to choose	"Given themselves over to sensuality" (Eph. 4:19)

Through Christ and God's grace, our relationship and right standing with the Lord can be restored. We can be justified by faith. Justification is a judge's pronouncement of a person's right standing before the law. We are no longer condemned (see Romans 8:1). When a judge condemns someone, he does not make the person a sinner; rather, he simply declares that such is the case. In justification, God is not making us inherently righteous; rather, He is declaring that we are in a right standing before His law. This change of legal relationship is a gift from God because of Christ's sacrifice on our behalf.

Out of the kindness of our Lord, our relationship has been restored. We have been set free from our sins. We are no longer children of wrath; we are children of God. We are no longer darkened in our understanding; we have been given the mind of Christ, and the Holy Spirit will lead us into all truth. We are no longer spiritually dead; we are alive in Christ. We are no longer hardened in our hearts; we have been given a new heart and a new spirit. We are no longer given over to sensuality; we have been given the freedom to live a morally pure life by the grace of God.

What is it like to stand before a judge when you both know you are guilty?

_____

_____

_____

What is the best sentence you could hope for once you have been found guilty?

_____

_____

_____

Who can rectify the guilty sentence? You or the judge? Why?

_____

_____

_____

Have you ever tried to defend yourself when you knew you were wrong? Did that work in the long term?

_____

_____

_____

_____

What defense mechanisms have you employed to defend yourself (lying, blaming, hiding)?

_____

_____

_____

After having taught what conflict there is in those who are caught in the struggle between a mind which lives according to the law of God and the desires of the flesh which lead them to sin [Romans 7], Paul now goes on to talk not about those who are partly in the flesh and partly in the Spirit, but about those who are wholly in Christ. He declares that there is nothing in them worthy of condemnation [Romans 8:1].

Origen (AD 184–253)

3

Peace With God

Judges 6:1–24

Key Point

Because we have been justified through faith, we have peace with God through our Lord Jesus Christ.

Key Verse

He came and preached peace to you who were far away and peace to those who were near.

Ephesians 2:17

When the angel of the LORD appeared to Gideon, he said, 'The LORD is with you, mighty warrior'" (Judges 6:12). The angel of the Lord was probably a "theophany" (a manifestation of God) or a pre-incarnate appearance of Christ. Like Moses, Gideon had been commissioned by God to deliver Israel. To make sure this word was from God, Gideon asked for a sign (see verse 17).

So it was that when Gideon brought his offering as instructed, an amazing miracle occurred. "Fire flared from the rock, consuming the meat and the bread. . . . When Gideon realized that it was the angel of the LORD, he exclaimed, 'Alas, Sovereign LORD! I have seen the angel of the LORD face to face!' But the Lord said to him, 'Peace! Do not be afraid. You are not going to die'" (verses 21–23).

Any unregenerate person would respond as Gideon did if suddenly confronted by the presence of God. That being the case, why would anybody want to draw near to a holy God who is perceived as a consuming fire? That is the unfortunate perspective of many defeated Christians. They live as though God were out to get them. If they make just one mistake, they think the hammer of God will surely fall on them.

Dear child of God, the hammer fell. It fell on Christ, once and for all. You are not a sinner in the hands of an angry God. You are a saint in the hands of a loving God who has called you to come before His presence. "In him and through faith in him we may approach God with freedom and confidence" (Ephesians 3:12).

"So Gideon built an altar to the LORD there and called it The LORD Is Peace" (verse 24). Jesus is the Prince of Peace, and His primary work has been to mediate peace between fallen humanity and God. "Now in Christ Jesus you who once were far away have been brought near through the blood of Christ" (Ephesians 2:13). Peace is now no longer out of reach: "Therefore, since we have been justified through faith, we have peace with God through our Lord Jesus Christ" (Romans 5:1). Paul describes this justification—this peace between God and humankind—using the past tense. It has already been accomplished. There is nothing more that needs to be done. We will not die in the presence of God as Gideon feared. We are already in the presence of God, because we are alive "in Him."

As the Peacemaker, Jesus also reconciles Jew and Gentile, "For he himself is our peace, who has made the two groups one and has destroyed the barrier, the dividing wall of hostility, by setting aside in his flesh the law with its commands and regulations. His purpose was to create in himself one new humanity out of the two, thus making peace, and in one body to reconcile both of them to God through the cross, by which he put to death their hostility" (Ephesians 2:14–16).

When the barrier between God and us is torn down in Christ, it also brings down the barrier between those who are committed to Him. Trying to negotiate peace in this world without first having peace with God has not proven successful. Peace between religious and philosophical factions can only happen when both find their peace with the same God.

How did Gideon respond when confronted by the presence of God? In what ways do many Christians respond the same way?

Why don't some Christians sense the peace to "approach God with freedom and confidence"?

In what ways has Jesus been the Prince of Peace?

Do you feel at peace living in the presence of God? Why or why not?

What relationship do you need to restore?

<hr>

Faith gives us peace with God, not the law. For it reconciles us to God by taking away those sins which had made us God's enemies. And because the Lord Jesus is the minister of this grace, it is through Him that we have peace with God. Faith is greater than the law, because the law is our work, whereas faith belongs to God. Furthermore, the law is concerned with our present life, whereas faith is concerned with eternal life. But whoever does not think this way about Christ, as he ought to, will not be able to obtain the rewards of faith, because he does not hold the truth of faith.

Ambrosiaster (written c. AD 366–384)

4

Access to God

Hebrews 10:19–25

Key Point

We have complete access to God through our Lord Jesus Christ.

Key Verse

In him and through faith in him we may approach God with freedom and confidence.

Ephesians 3:12

Who may ascend the mountain of the LORD? Who may stand in his holy place? He who has clean hands and a pure heart" (Psalm 24:3–4). Jesus said it is the "pure in heart" who will see God and experience fellowship with Him (see Matthew 5:8). Because we have all sinned and fallen short of the glory of God (see Romans 3:23), who can approach Him?

In the Old Testament, everything about the Temple was set up to emphasize the near-unapproachable holiness and power of God. Only priests could enter the Temple, and only the high priest on one day a year—the Day of Atonement—could go into the Holy of Holies behind a thick veil or curtain that separated God from the priests. This was a day of great fear, reverence, and awe. The high priest entered only after going through a great deal of ceremonial cleansing. Even then, he probably entered with fear and trepidation, not knowing if he would come out alive. The other priests actually tied a rope around his ankles to pull him out of God's presence if it appeared that he had expired, because nobody else wanted to go in after him.

In the New Testament, there is a radical shift in access to God. The moment Jesus died for our sins on the cross, "The curtain of the temple was torn in two from top to bottom" (Mark 15:38). The relationship between God and humankind had been restored. As the writer of Hebrews says, "We have confidence to enter the Most Holy Place by the blood of Jesus, by a new and living way opened for us through the curtain, that is, his body and since we have a great priest over the house of God, let us draw near to God with a sincere heart in full assurance of faith, having our hearts sprinkled to cleanse us from a guilty conscience and having our bodies washed with pure water" (Hebrews 10:19–22).

Suppose you petitioned for months to have an audience with the president of the United States. Finally, you were granted your request and given 15 minutes alone with him. Since you have no personal relationship with him, what would you hope to gain by such a visit?

Now suppose that you had access to the God who created the president of the United States. He has even taken the initiative to invite you into His presence (see Matthew 11:28). You know this God personally, and He has known you from the foundations of the world. You have an audience with Him 24 hours of every day, and He listens to you. "This is the confidence we have in approaching God: that if we ask anything according to his will, he hears us" (1 John 5:14).

Knowing that we have access to God, let us never lose hope (see Hebrews 10:23). We have a God of all hope, and with Him all things are possible. So if you are discouraged, draw near to God and you will find mercy and grace in time of need (see Hebrews 4:16). Because we have access to God, "let us consider how we may spur one another on toward love and good deeds, not giving up meeting together . . . but encouraging one another" (Hebrews 10:24–25).

Who could approach God in the Old Testament?

How did the high priest enter the Holy of Holies? Why did he likely enter that place with fear and trepidation?

What was the significance of the veil in the Temple being torn down that separated God from the people? How do you think the people would have responded at the time?

How does knowing that you have complete access to an all-powerful, all-knowing, and all-loving God fill you with hope for the future?

What right do you have to enter the Holy of Holies?

_____

_____

_____

"Let us draw near," he [the writer of Hebrews] says, "with a true heart." To the holy things, the faith, the spiritual service. "With a true heart, in full assurance of faith," since nothing is seen, neither the priest henceforth, not the sacrifice, not the altar. And yet neither was the Old Testament priest visible, but stood within, and they all without, the whole people. But here not only has this taken place, that the priest has entered into the Holy of Holies, but that we also enter in.

John Chrysostom (AD 347–407)

5

The Coming of the Holy Spirit

Joel 2:28–32

Key Point

The Church Era began when the Holy Spirit was poured out on all believers, fulfilling the prophecy of Joel.

Key Verse

I will pour out my Spirit on all people.

Joel 2:28

On the Day of Pentecost, the followers of Jesus were gathered together in the Upper Room in Jerusalem. They were following Jesus' instructions to "not leave Jerusalem, but wait for the gift my Father promised" (Acts 1:4). Suddenly, "a sound like the blowing of a violent wind came from heaven and filled the whole house where they were sitting. They saw what seemed to be tongues of fire that separated and came to rest on each of them. All of them were filled with the Holy Spirit and began to speak in other tongues as the Spirit enabled them" (2:2–4). Peter

103

immediately associated those spiritual manifestations with the fulfillment of Joel's prophecy (see verses 16–21; Joel 2:28–32).

The coming of the Holy Spirit at Pentecost is what distinguishes the Old Covenant from the New Covenant. Prior to Pentecost, the presence of God was *with* His people. In the Church Age after Pentecost, the presence of God is now *within* believers in the person of the Holy Spirit. Old Testament believers had a legal relationship with God, but New Testament believers have a new identity and a personal relationship with their heavenly Father. The primary work of the Holy Spirit is to testify "with our spirit that we are God's children" (Romans 8:16). Peter wrote, "Once you were not a people, but now you are the people of God; once you had not received mercy, but now you have received mercy" (1 Peter 2:10).

Through the prophet Joel, God said, "I will pour out my Spirit on all people" (Joel 2:28). This universal inclusion of all people is also a marked difference between the Old and the New Testament. God said that "all peoples on earth will be blessed" (Genesis 12:3) through the seed of Abraham. This will be true regardless of race, age, gender, or social class (see Joel 2:29). "And everyone who calls on the name of the LORD will be saved" (verse 32; see also Romans 10:13).

In the Old Testament, God spoke through the prophets to the people, but in the Church Age, God personally leads every one of His children, "for those who are led by the Spirit of God are the children of God" (Romans 8:14). In the Old Testament, Moses said, "I wish that all the LORD's people were prophets and that the LORD would put his Spirit on them" (Numbers 11:29). God has put His Spirit in every New Testament believer, and according to Joel's prophecy, "Your sons and daughters will prophesy, your old men will dream dreams, your young men will see visions" (2:28). Because of our personal relationship with God, He will uniquely equip all His children.

Generally speaking, the "day of the LORD" (verse 31) is an idiom used to emphasize the decisive nature of God's victory over His enemies. Prior to Pentecost, Jesus defeated the devil; and according to Paul, it is the eternal purpose of God to make His wisdom known through the Church to the rulers and authorities in the heavenly realms, which is the spiritual kingdom of darkness (see Ephesians 3:10–12). The enemy knows he is defeated when the children of God speak the truth in love through the power of the Holy Spirit.

In what ways does the coming of the Holy Spirit at Pentecost distinguish the Old Covenant from the New Covenant?

Many of those who were present at Pentecost had witnessed the crucifixion and resurrection of Christ. So why were they instructed to wait in Jerusalem before they could be witnesses?

What defines the Church today?

How has the Holy Spirit empowered your life to be a witness?

Of what are you a witness?

_____

_____

_____

_____

He [Jesus] said earlier, "Go nowhere among the Gentiles, and enter no town of the Samaritans." What He did not say then, He added here [Acts 1:8], "and to the ends of the earth." "When He said this, as they were watching, He was lifted up, and a cloud took Him out of their sight." . . . For they saw in the resurrection the end, but not the beginning, and they saw in the ascension the beginning, but not the end.

John Chrysostom (AD 347–407)

Effective Prayer

What humans cannot do in eternity, God can do in an instant, and He does it in response to our prayers. Scottish minister Thomas Chalmers said, "Prayer does not enable us to do a greater work for God. Prayer is a greater work for God." The prophet Samuel demonstrated this principle when he said, "Now then, stand still and see this great thing the LORD is about to do before your eyes" (1 Samuel 12:16). God didn't move until "Samuel called on the LORD" (verse 18).

James said, "The prayer of a righteous person is powerful and effective. Elijah was a human being, even as we are. He prayed earnestly that it would not rain, and it did not rain on the land for three and a half years. Again he prayed, and the heavens gave rain, and the earth produced its crops" (5:16–18). Both Samuel and Elijah were righteous, which is why they were effective in prayer. However, in every other way they were no different from us.

We will never be effective in prayer if we go to God only in emergencies and then return to managing our own lives when the crisis passes. That would make prayer a fourth-down punting situation instead of a first-down huddle. It is not appropriate to ask God to bless our plans; we must humbly ask God to reveal His plans. God is capable of doing anything that is consistent with His nature. The question is, will He? We may never know unless we ask. Prayer is not conquering God's reluctance. It is laying hold of God's willingness. "This is the confidence we have in approaching God: that if we ask anything according to his will, he hears us. And if we know that he hears us—whatever we ask—we know that we have what we asked of him" (1 John 5:14–15). Our prayers will always be effective if our petitions and intercessions are in agreement with the Word of God.

Paul instructed us to be alert and pray in the Spirit for all the saints (see Ephesians 6:18). Prayer is part of our divine protection as believers. We need to respond immediately in prayer to the Spirit's prompting and to the requests of our brothers and sisters in Christ. In addition, Paul says, "I urge, then, first of all, that requests, prayers, intercession and thanksgiving be made for all people—for kings and all those in authority, that we may live peaceful and quiet lives in all godliness and holiness" (1 Timothy 2:1–2).

Samuel considered it a sin against God not to pray for others (see 1 Samuel 12:23). However, we can only ask the Lord to do through others what we are willing for the Lord to do through us. Only to the degree that we have been tested and found approved can we request on behalf of others. Neither Christ nor the Holy Spirit can intercede through us on a higher level than that which they have first had victory in us. Christ is the perfect intercessor because He took the place of each one prayed for.

A New Humanity

In the Old West, a circuit preacher came upon an orphaned boy named Peter. He realized that he couldn't raise the boy and continue his ministry, so he looked for someone who could. He heard of a Christian couple named Mr. and Mrs. Smith. They had a little boy named Sammy who was about Peter's age.

The couple agreed to raise Peter, and the boys became the best of friends. Sammy was an obedient child, but Peter was incorrigible. One time, they told the boys not to swim in a contaminated pond on their property, but Peter went anyway. Peter must have scratched himself on some barbed wire, because he got sick. He was so sick that he had to be quarantined.

The Smiths had to make a trip to town and told Sammy not to go into Peter's room, lest he get sick as well. However, when they came home they found the two boys fast asleep in each other's arms. Nobody understands the providential care of God, but in this case Peter got well while Sammy got sick. In fact, Sammy died.

Several years passed before the circuit preacher made his way back to the farm where he had dropped off Peter. As he rode his horse up to the farmhouse, he recognized Mr. Smith, but not the young man standing beside him. "Say, whatever happened to that kid I dropped off several years ago," asked the preacher. Mr. Smith put his arm over the shoulders of the young man. "Meet Peter Smith," he said. "We have adopted him. He is my son and part of the Smith family."

Daily Readings

1. A New Family	Ephesians 4:1–16
2. A New Covenant	Jeremiah 31:23–34
3. A New Creation	2 Corinthians 5:11–21
4. A New Heart	Proverbs 4:20–27
5. A New Spirit	John 3:1–15

1

A New Family

Ephesians 4:1–16

Key Point

Fellowship in the family of God affirms our identity in Christ.

Key Verses

But you are a chosen people, a royal priesthood, a holy nation, God's special possession, that you may declare the praises of him who called you out of darkness into his wonderful light. Once you were not a people, but now you are the people of God; once you had not received mercy, but now you have received mercy.

1 Peter 2:9–10

In sanctification we not only "participate in the divine nature" (2 Peter 1:4) but also allow God to restore our true nature as human beings. The true nature of humanity is realized in Christian community. An individual becomes fully human only in relationship to God and His people. It is clear from God's statement that "it is not good for the man to be alone" (Genesis 2:18) that we as humans were not designed to live in isolation from others. To be human is to be co-human.

Our community nature as humans is also evident from the fact that we were created in the image of God, who is triune. The Trinity is a fellowship of three persons, making God a social being. The Father would not be the Father except for His relationship to the Son and the Spirit. The Son would not be the Son without being related to the Father and the Spirit.

We exist, then, not as separate entities but as a part of humanity. The Bible's often-used metaphor of the Church as a body makes this apparent. If we were to find a part that was separated from the rest of the body and we have no knowledge of its relation to the body, we would be unable to identify what it really was—its nature, purpose, and function. A toe or kneecap by itself would appear to serve no useful purpose. We would simply identify it as a useless blob of flesh. It acquires its identity only in relation to other parts of the body. We not only have a personal relationship with God but, being part of the family of God, we also have a corporate relationship with our heavenly Father.

We require community to know fulfillment as humans, and our Christian growth also requires community for us to reach our full God-designed potential as born-again humans. To accomplish this, God "gave the apostles, the prophets, the evangelists, the pastors and teachers, to equip his people for works of service, so that the Body of Christ may be built up until we all reach unity in the faith and in the knowledge of the Son of God and become mature, attaining to the whole measure of the fullness of Christ" (Ephesians 4:11–13). We absolutely need God, and we necessarily need each other.

When we come to Christ, we come with all the others who are alive in Christ. Paul wrote, "There is neither Jew nor Gentile, neither slave nor free, nor is there male and female, for you are all one in Christ Jesus" (Galatians 3:28). This oneness is expressed repeatedly in the book of Ephesians. We are all "fellow citizens" (2:19). We are "joined together . . . to become a holy temple in the Lord" and "built together to become a dwelling in which God lives by his Spirit" (2:21–22). The gospel has made us all "heirs together," "members together," and "sharers together" (3:6).

Solitary sainthood is unknown to the New Testament. Sanctification is not just a matter of *I* or *me*. The New Testament commonly speaks of holiness using the terms "we" and "our." The word "saint" is used 60 times in the plural, but only once in the singular. Therefore, dear Christian, welcome to the family of God.

Can a believer have a good relationship with God in exclusion of other believers? Explain.

_____

_____

_____

_____

How does fellowship in the family of God affirm our true identity in Christ?

_____

_____

_____

In what ways are we in need of each other?

_____

_____

_____

How is your relationship with God being helped or hindered by other believers?

_____

_____

_____

_____

Do you presently sense that you are part of the family of God? Why or why not?

_____

_____

_____

This title of honor [see 1 Peter 2:9], which God gave to His ancient people through Moses, the apostle Peter now applies to the Gentiles, and rightly so, because they have believed in Christ who was the true cornerstone of Israel's faith. The Gentiles are therefore a chosen race, in contradistinction to those who have been rejected because they themselves rejected the living stone. They are a royal priesthood because they are joined to the body of Him who is both the king and the true high priest. As their king, Christ grants them a share in His kingdom and as their priest He purifies them with the sacrifice of His own blood.

Bede (AD 673–735)

2

A New Covenant

Jeremiah 31:23–34

Key Point

Under the New Covenant of grace, we live by faith in the power of the Holy Spirit.

Key Verse

I will put my law in their minds and write it on their hearts. I will be their God, and they will be my people.

Jeremiah 31:33

God made a covenant with the nation of Israel at the time of the Exodus from Egypt. This conditional Mosaic Covenant (detailed in the books of Exodus, Leviticus, Numbers, and Deuteronomy) stipulated that the Israelites would receive God's blessings if they obeyed Him but would be punished if they didn't (see Leviticus 26; Deuteronomy 28). Because they disobeyed and rebelled against the Law, their final judgment came with the fall of Jerusalem in 586 BC. The Temple was destroyed and the Jewish people were deported to Babylon, where they remained in captivity for 70 years.

However, God had not forgotten His people. Through the prophet Jeremiah, God made a new covenant with the Israelites. God said, "I will put my law in their minds and write it on their hearts. I will be their God, and they will be my people" (Jeremiah 31:33). According to this New Covenant, God's law would be written on their hearts rather than on stone tablets (see Exodus 34:1). They would have the ability to live up to His righteous standards and enjoy His blessings because of the indwelling presence of the Holy Spirit.

This New Covenant also made a provision for our sin. God said, "I will forgive their wickedness and will remember their sins no more" (Jeremiah 31:34). By making this covenant, God was not overlooking our sin, nor was He forgetting it. God couldn't forget it, because He is omniscient. "I will remember your sins no more" means "I will not take the past and use it against you in the future." Psalm 103:12 says, "As far as the east is from the west, so far has he removed our transgressions from us."

In order for the New Covenant to be efficacious, a sacrifice would be required. Before His crucifixion, Jesus announced in the Upper Room that the New Covenant would be inaugurated through the shedding of His blood (see Matthew 26:27–28; Luke 22:20). The permanence of this New Covenant was underscored by the promise that the descendants of Israel would continue to exist (see Jeremiah 31:35–36). The power God displayed in creating the universe was the same power that would ensure the preservation of His Chosen People.

Although this covenant was made with Israel and Judah (see Jeremiah 31:31), the Church would also receive the benefits of it (see Hebrews 8:8–12). The New Covenant was inaugurated on the Day of Pentecost when all the Jewish believers were gathered to celebrate the fiftieth day after the Sabbath of Passover week. Thus, the Early Church believers were all Jewish. John wrote, "Salvation is from the Jews" (John 4:22), and the unconditional covenant God had made with Abraham ensured that "all peoples on earth" would be blessed through Abraham (Genesis 12:3). As the book of Acts tells us, the gospel first came to the Jews and then to the Gentiles.

The Church has been grafted into the original "branch," which is Israel (see Romans 11). All New Testament believers, both Jew and Gentile, live under the New Covenant that guarantees spiritual life and the forgiveness of sins. Consequently, believers no longer relate to God on the basis of the old Mosaic Covenant that required strict observance of the Law. The New Covenant is one of grace that calls for believers to live by faith in the power of the Holy Spirit.

What were the terms and conditions of the old Mosaic Covenant that God established with Israel?

How was the law a taskmaster that would lead us to Christ?

How are Gentiles included with Israel in the New Covenant?

How would you describe your relationship with God in terms of law or grace?

How have you personally struggled with legalism?

_____

_____

_____

Inasmuch as the apostle says to the Hebrews, "A will takes effect only at the death of the one who made it," he therefore asserts that, with Christ's death for us, the new covenant has become valid. Its likeness was the old covenant, in which the death of the testator was prefigured in the sacrificial victim. Therefore, if one should ask how it is that we, in the word of the same apostle, are "Children and heirs of God and fellow heirs with Christ," since of course the inheritance is made valid by the death of the deceased and since an inheritance cannot be understood in any other way, the answer is this: He Himself having in fact died, we have become heirs because we were also called His sons.

Augustine of Hippo (AD 354–430)

3

A New Creation

2 Corinthians 5:11–21

Key Point

We have been grafted into Christ, and He will prune away our old nature that doesn't bear fruit.

Key Verse

All this is from God, who reconciled us to himself through Christ and gave us the ministry of reconciliation.

2 Corinthians 5:18

As born-again believers, we are all new creations in Christ. Although we may not always feel like it or act like it, Scripture clearly teaches that we have a new identity: we are children of God (see 1 John 3:1–3) and no longer children of wrath (see Ephesians 2:1–3). This immediate spiritual transformation and continuing growth will be easier for us to understand if we are familiar with a particular agricultural technique that is used in the semitropical climate zones where a frost can severely damage citrus crops.

In these regions, horticulturists have learned to use the bitter-tasting ornamental orange as rootstock because it can take a moderate freeze without damage. When the ornamental orange tree has grown to the right stage, they cut the stem just above the ground and graft in a sweet orange, such as a navel orange. The new growth above the graft has a new nature.

Nobody looks at a navel orange grove and says, "Actually, all those trees are nothing but rootstock." They were at one time, but they no longer are. Now, people identify the orchard by the type of fruit the trees are bearing. The same is true for us. Jesus said, "By their fruit you will recognize them" (Matthew 7:16). Believers are identified for who they are "in Christ," not for who they were "in Adam."

"Suckers," or small green sprouts, can continue to grow from the old roots, but they need to be trimmed off. If they are allowed to grow, they will divert the growth of the tree away from the new graft. In the same way, the gardener cuts off every branch that does not bear fruit and prunes every branch that is bearing fruit so it may bear even more (see John 15:2).

We have been grafted into Christ, and He will prune away our old nature that doesn't bear fruit. This transformation from who we were "in Adam" to who we are now "in Christ" may be summarized as follows:

In Adam		In Christ
Old self (Col. 3:9)	*by birth*	New self (Col. 3:10)
Sin nature (Eph. 2:1–3)	*by nature*	Participate in the divine nature (2 Pet. 1:4)
Live according to the sinful nature (flesh; Rom. 8:5a)	*by choice*	Live in accordance with the Spirit or flesh (Rom. 8:5b; Gal. 5:13–23)

The apostle Paul consistently identifies the believers according to who they are in Christ and never identifies them by their old nature/flesh. "From now on, therefore, we regard no one according to the flesh" (2 Corinthians 5:16 ESV). In other words, we shouldn't perceive other believers as natural people who derive their identity from their physical origin and natural existence.

Returning to the tree illustration, that which grows above the graft has only one nature, but the total tree has two natures (rootstock and navel). The believer still lives in a mortal body and is confronted with the choice of living according to the old sinful nature (flesh) or according to the Spirit.

However, the apostle Paul says, "Those who belong to Christ Jesus have crucified the sinful nature with its passions and desires" (Galatians 5:24). We are new creations in Christ, and we belong to Him. Someday, we will leave our physical body, receive a resurrected body, and live forever—with only one righteous nature—in the presence of God.

When a navel orange is grafted into an ornamental orange, the tree takes on a new identity. How is the same true when we are grafted into Christ?

Small green sprouts called "suckers" can divert the growth of a tree from the new graft. How is this similar to what can happen in our lives?

Why shouldn't believers identify themselves as sinners, alcoholics, addicts, co-dependents, and the like?

In what way is God pruning your life so that you may bear more fruit?

121

What labels have you worn that are not consistent with who you really are?

_____

_____

_____

We ought to live for Christ not just because we belong to Him, not just because He died for us and not just because He rose again on our behalf. We ought to live for Him because we have been made into something different. We now have a new life. Old things which have passed away refer to our sins and impiety, as well as all the observances of Judaism.

John Chrysostom (AD 347–407)

4

A New Heart

Proverbs 4:20–27

Key Point

God is trying to enlarge our hearts and not just our minds.

Key Verse

*I will give them a heart to know me, that I am the L*ORD.

Jeremiah 24:7

zekiel prophesied, "I will give them an undivided heart and put a new spirit in them; I will remove from them their heart of stone and give them a heart of flesh. Then they will follow my decrees and be careful to keep my laws. They will be my people, and I will be their God" (Ezekiel 11:19–20). A new heart and a new spirit are clearly gifts from God. Jeremiah prophesied, "I will give them a heart to know me, that I am the LORD. They will be my people, and I will be their God, for they will return to me with all their heart" (Jeremiah 24:7). This is a heart to know and experience God.

123

Contrary to popular thinking, emotion is not the dominant function of the heart. H. Wheeler Robinson, an Oxford academic, analyzed the functions of the heart in his book *The Christian Doctrine of Man*. Robinson counted 822 uses of the word "heart" in Scripture when used in reference to human personality. According to his categorization, 204 of the 822 uses refer to our intellect, 195 to our will, and 166 to our emotions.[1] It is better to think of our heart as the center of self and the seat of reflection rather than just the seat of our emotions.

The essential business of the heart is stated in Proverbs 15:14: "The discerning heart seeks knowledge." The word for "heart" occurs most frequently in the portions of the Bible known as the wisdom literature (for example, 99 times in Proverbs and 42 times in Ecclesiastes) as well as the highly instructional book of Deuteronomy (51 times). These portions of Scripture instruct us in the way of God's wisdom, which we are to know and understand with our hearts. Thus, the goal of life is to gain a heart of wisdom. "Teach us to number our days, that we may gain a heart of wisdom" (Psalm 90:12).

The truth of God's Word must penetrate our hearts in order for it to direct our ways and transform our lives. It is possible to intellectually know the truth and yet not allow it to have an impact on how we feel or what we do. Only in the heart do the mind, emotion, and will come together in holistic unity. When we allow the truth to penetrate our hearts, it immediately stirs the emotions, which drives the will. The biblical idea of knowing God and knowing the truth that will set us free involves our emotions and our will, not just our intellect. To grow and live righteous lives, we must experience God, not just have an intellectual knowledge of His attributes.

Many believers are not experiencing God's presence or the liberating benefits of knowing Him because they have never gotten beyond an intellectual understanding of who He is. The greatest commandment is to "love the Lord your God with all your heart and with all your soul and with all your mind" (Matthew 22:37). God is trying to enlarge our hearts, not just our minds. The Truth has to be incarnated and become a living Word within us, and that is possible because the indwelling Jesus is the Truth and the Word.

What does it mean to have a new heart that knows and experiences God?

According to God's Word, what is the heart?

The goal of life is to attain a heart of wisdom. How is that different from a head full of knowledge?

What evidence have you sensed in your own life that confirms the truth that you have a new heart?

How have you gone beyond simple "head" knowledge of Christ and allowed Him to enlarge your heart?

_____

_____

_____

Therefore the first commandment teaches every kind of godliness. For to love God with the whole heart is the cause of every good. The second commandment includes the righteous acts we do toward other people. The first commandment prepares the way for the second and in turn is established by the second. For the person who is grounded in the love of God clearly also loves his neighbor in all things himself. The kind of person who fulfills those two commandments experiences all the commandments.

Cyril of Alexandria (AD 376–444)

5

A New Spirit

John 3:1–15

Key Point

The Holy Spirit has taken up residence in our bodies and made them temples of God.

Key Verse

Do you not know that your bodies are temples of the Holy Spirit, who is in you, whom you have received from God? You are not your own.

1 Corinthians 6:19

Nicodemus was a Pharisee and a member of the Sanhedrin. Not wanting his colleagues to know of his association with Jesus, Nicodemus went to see Him under the cover of darkness to inquire about the kingdom of God. He recognized that Jesus taught with authority, and he knew that no one could have performed the miracles that Jesus had unless God were with Him. He told Jesus, "Rabbi, we know that you are a teacher who has come from God. For no one could perform the signs you are doing if God were not with him" (John 3:1–2).

Jesus turned the conversation to the doctrine of regeneration. He replied, "Very truly I tell you, no one can see the kingdom of God unless they are born again" (verse 3). Nicodemus did not understand—he wondered how a child could again enter into the womb of his mother. However, Jesus was not talking about going through the natural birth process again; rather, He was talking about a new birth.

What distinguishes the natural birth from this new spiritual birth is its origin. "Flesh gives birth to flesh, but the Spirit gives birth to spirit" (John 3:6). The term "born again" literally means "born from above." In regeneration, the supernatural origin is just as important as the newness of the birth. The ideas of "newness," "regeneration," and a supernatural origin are all joined together in Titus 3:5–6: "He saved us through the washing of rebirth and renewal by the Holy Spirit, whom he poured out on us generously through Jesus Christ our Savior."

In salvation, there is a washing and a renewing—a change in the innermost attitudes and inclinations of our hearts of such a nature that it can only be compared with the generation and birth of life. Unlike natural birth, however, this birth does not have its origin in the will of humankind but in the sovereign power of God. It is a birth that is not of the flesh, nor of blood, but of the Spirit.

In regeneration, the Holy Spirit indwells every believer. His coming produces a radical change from pollution and death to holiness and life. The coming of the Holy Spirit produces a new creation in Christ. The newly "born from above" believer is exhorted to "put on the new self, created to be like God in true righteousness and holiness" (Ephesians 4:24). Even as newborn children cannot orchestrate their own conception and birth, neither can believers take any credit for the transformation of their lives. The power to change comes from above.

Unregenerate people are like dry sponges wrapped in plastic. In that state, they serve no useful purpose. Then one day, God strips away the plastic wrapping, puts the squeeze on them, and plunges them into a pool of His living water. While they are submerged God loosens His grip, and every pore of their being is filled with His presence. Now they are complete in Christ and able to fulfill the purpose for which they were created. Should these sponges decide to pull away from the water, they would soon dry out and fail again to fulfill their purpose, even though they are forever free from that which originally bound them.

Born-again believers are Holy Spirit possessed—the Holy Spirit has taken up residence in their bodies and made them temples of God.

How did Jesus distinguish natural birth from spiritual birth? What did He mean when He told Nicodemus he must be "born again"?

_____

_____

_____

What does "regeneration" mean?

_____

_____

_____

How are unregenerate people like "dry sponges wrapped in plastic"? What happens when they are born again?

_____

_____

_____

What does it mean to you that your body is a temple of God and a dwelling place for the Almighty?

_____

_____

_____

What is keeping you from taking in God's goodness like a dry sponge?

_____

_____

_____

_____

What is Paul trying to prove when he says that we are not our own? He wants to secure us against sin and against following the improper desires of the mind. We have many improper desires, but we must constrain them, and we can do so. If we could not, there would be no point in exhorting us like this. Paul does not say that we are under compulsion but that we have been bought—and bought with a great price, reminding us of the way in which our salvation was obtained.

John Chrysostom (AD 347–407)

Praying for the Lost

In Jonah 1, God told the prophet Jonah to go to Nineveh and preach, but he refused. Jonah knew that God would spare the Ninevites if they repented, and he did not want these enemies of Israel to be spared. Because of his disobedience, he found himself in the belly of a fish praying for his own salvation (see Jonah 2). Jonah did go to Nineveh, and to his disappointment the people repented and God relented (see Jonah 3).

Sensing his anger at the outcome, God gave Jonah an object lesson through a leafy plant that withered and died (see Jonah 4). If Jonah was justified in being upset about the loss of a plant to whose existence he had contributed nothing, was not God justified in showing love and concern for the people of Nineveh, whom He created?

130

The story of Jonah forces us to examine our hearts. Do we want the judgment of God to fall on all the lost people of this world, or do we want them to repent and believe? If the lost are our enemies, the question becomes a test of our character. Do we have a heart like Jonah, or do we have a heart like God? We are not all called to be full-time missionaries or evangelists, but we are called to share our faith and pray. There are two principles that we need to know in order to effectively pray for the lost.

First, Jesus said, "The harvest is plentiful but the workers are few. Ask the Lord of the harvest, therefore, to send out workers into his harvest field" (Matthew 9:37–38). If you have a burden to pray for someone or some group of people who don't know the Lord, ask God to send them a messenger. God has to work through His established means of bringing salvation to the lost people of this world. In Romans 10:14–15, Paul explains what that process is: "How, then, can they call on the one they have not believed in? And how can they believe in the one of whom they have not heard? And how can they hear without someone preaching to them? And how can anyone preach unless they are sent?"

Second, John wrote, "If you see any brother or sister commit a sin that does not lead to death, you should pray and God will give them life" (1 John 5:16). The context of this passage is clearly talking about spiritual life and death, not physical life and death. The lost people of this world are dead in their trespasses and sins. Jesus came that we might have life. So John is telling us to petition God to give them eternal life. Our prayers do not save them; they are saved by their own personal faith in the finished work of Christ. However, in His sovereignty, God has chosen to work out His plan of salvation through the Church. We choose to believe, but God saves us. God miraculously works in response to our prayers, including the salvation of souls.

A New Beginning

A Christian recovery group was just beginning its weekly meeting when a guest speaker was introduced. The speaker took a $20 bill out of his pocket and asked if anyone would like to have it. Many raised their hands.

"I'm going to give it away this evening," he said, "but first let me do this." He proceeded to crumple the bill in his hand. "Who still wants this $20 bill?" he asked. The same hands went up.

"But what if I do this?" he asked. He dropped the bill to the floor and started grinding on it with his shoe. He picked up the crumpled dirty bill and asked again if anyone wanted it. The same hands went up.

He gave the bill to the newest person in the group and said, "No matter what I did to the bill, you still wanted it—and rightly so, because it still had the same value, no matter how it was abused. We all have been dropped, crumpled, and ground into the dirt by the decisions we made and the circumstances that came our way. Consequently, we feel as though we are worthless, but that is not true. Your value as a human being, created in the image of God, will never lose its value no matter what happened to you or what you have done. You are not a derelict, you are not a bum, you are not an alcoholic, you are not an addict. You are a child of God, and just like the newest member of your group, you did nothing to earn the free gift of salvation. My gift only cost me $20; the gift of salvation cost Jesus His life."

Daily Readings

1. Overcoming Guilt	Romans 8:1–8
2. Overcoming Shame	Micah 7:7–10
3. Conviction of Sin	2 Corinthians 7:2–12
4. Our Inheritance in Christ	Hebrews 1:1–4
5. The Love of Christ	Ephesians 3:14–21

1

Overcoming Guilt

Romans 8:1–8

Key Point

There is no condemnation for those who are in Christ Jesus our Lord.

Key Verse

Through Christ Jesus the law of the Spirit who gives life has set you free from the law of sin and death.

Romans 8:2

Guilt is a judicial concept in a court of law presided over by a judge. In order to establish guilt or innocence, there has to be a law or moral standard. People are deemed guilty when they fail to live up to a moral standard or when they break the law. In the book of Romans, Paul argues our case for a "not guilty" verdict in the heavenly court where God is the presiding judge.

Paul starts by admitting that "there is no one righteous, not even one" (Romans 3:10), "for all have sinned and fall short of the glory of God"

(3:23). That is not the defense we were hoping for, but he isn't finished! "All are justified freely by his grace through the redemption that came by Jesus Christ" (3:24). Did God do away with the law or water it down so all would qualify on their own merit? A righteous judge couldn't do that, because justice must be served. So, "God presented Christ as a sacrifice of atonement, through the shedding of his blood—to be received in faith. He did this to demonstrate his righteousness" (3:25).

This infuriates the prosecutor, who accuses those who have sinned day and night (see Revelation 12:10). "Jesus couldn't have paid it all," whispers the evil one. He demands the judge make them earn their way. Paul argues back, "Now to the one who works, wages are not credited as a gift but as an obligation. However, to the one who does not work but trusts God who justifies the ungodly, their faith is credited as righteousness" (Romans 4:4–5). "Therefore, since we have been justified through faith, we have peace with God through our Lord Jesus Christ" (5:1).

Paul then turns to the accused and says, "Count yourselves dead to sin but alive to God in Christ Jesus" (6:11). *I would like to do that*, says the doubter, *but sin is still all around me, and believing Christians are still dying.* Paul explains that death is the end of a relationship but not of existence. Besides, "sin shall no longer be your master, because you are not under the law, but under grace" (6:14). Under the law Satan had a standard by which he could accuse the person, but under grace he doesn't. "Therefore, there is now no condemnation for those who are in Christ Jesus, because through Christ Jesus the law of the Spirit who gives life has set you free from the law of sin and death" (8:1–2).

Paul used the word "law" in reference to sin and death to make a powerful point. You can't do away with a law, so how can justified Christians overcome such laws? They overcome the law of sin and the law of death by a greater law, which is the law of life in Christ Jesus.

Have you ever tried to fly? You can't, because there is no power within you to overcome the law of gravity. However, we can "fly" in an airplane, which has the power to overcome the law of gravity. As long as we live by faith in the power of the Holy Spirit, we will not carry out the desires of the flesh (see Galatians 5:16).

"Not guilty," says the judge. Court adjourned.

Apart from Christ, why are we all guilty before God?

Why did justice have to be served?

How does one overcome the law of sin and the law of death?

How can you stand against the devil's accusations?

What power does sin and death have over you?

Paul holds out security for us by the grace of God, so that we should not be tempted by the suggestions of the devil. . . . We shall instead be rewarded if we repel the counsels of that sin which remains in us, for it demands great skill to avoid the tricks of the enemy. "The law of the Spirit of life" is the law of faith. For even the Law of Moses is spiritual in that it forbids us to sin, but it is not the law of life. It has no power to pardon those who are guilty of the sins which merit death and thus to bring them back to life. . . . Therefore it is the law in Christ Jesus, this is to say, through faith in Christ, which frees the believer from the law of sin and death.

Ambrosiaster (written c. AD 366–384)

2

Overcoming Shame

Micah 7:7–10

Key Point

True believers are motivated by the love of God and not by guilt and shame.

Key Verse

Hatred stirs up conflict, but love covers over all wrongs.

Proverbs 10:12

Christians are forgiven but not perfect. Jesus paid the penalty for our sins and assumed responsibility for their eternal consequences. As a result, the Lord will not condemn us and will remember our sins no more. However, we have to live with the temporal consequences of our attitudes and actions. If God had eradicated all the temporal consequences of sin, there would be no motivation to stop sinning. We would party on weekends, confess our sins on Sunday, and falsely believe that our actions have no negative consequences.

Suppose you have been consuming alcohol for years and have become chemically addicted. At first you were able to cover up your indiscretions, but now your sinful lifestyle has been exposed. Your job performance is substandard, you have embarrassed yourself publicly, your spouse has left, and your health is deteriorating. Finally, you throw yourself upon God's mercy. He forgives you and makes you a new creation in Christ. However, alcohol has taken its toll on your body. Your job is over, your spouse is gone, and you find that society is less forgiving than God. Still, you are able to find a successful recovery ministry that helps the fallen seek God's forgiveness, ask the forgiveness of others, repair what they can, and build a new life in Christ. The grace of God eventually overcomes your shame.

This was the case for Micah, who spoke to the sinful conditions of Israel and Judah. He looked forward to God's redemption—the coming of the Savior (see Micah 7:7)—even though he lived under the Mosaic Law. At the time, the Israelites' enemy was gloating over these "chosen people" who had sinned and incurred the judgment of God. Their enemy was taunting them, asking, "Where is the LORD your God?" (verse 10). Micah responds, "Though I have fallen, I will rise. Though I sit in darkness, the LORD will be my light" (verse 8). The shame the Israelites felt because of their sin caused them to hide and cover up, but the Lord always leads His people into the light. When they faced the truth and turned to God, their enemy was covered with shame, and its downfall was certain (see verse 10).

Many cultures of this world are shame-based. They punish sinners by shaming them publicly. They make the point that something is wrong with them. Other cultures are guilt-based. They punish sinners because they have done something wrong. The kingdom of God is grace-based. There was something wrong with us, but now we are new creations in Christ. We sinned and fell short of the glory of God, but Christ died for our sins. Now we can live righteous lives as children of God. We are what we are by the grace of God. We can still choose to sin, and our loving heavenly Father will discipline us, but that just proves that we are His children (see Hebrews 12:8).

As children of God, we are not motivated by guilt and shame. Piling on guilt and shame is detrimental to our mental health and doesn't promote righteous living. We are motivated by the love of God. We don't condemn others when they sin; we discipline them for their good. The Christian ministry is one of reconciliation, not condemnation. We don't shame one another; we build up one another.

What would happen to Christians and our culture if people never had to suffer temporal consequences for their sinful or irresponsible choices?

How can Christians overcome a sense of guilt and shame?

How is the kingdom of God grace-based instead of shame-based or guilt-based? What should be our motivations as new creations in Christ?

How have you allowed the shame of your past to keep you from moving forward in God's will? What steps will you take to change this pattern?

How has God disciplined you for sinful behavior? Did you see His discipline as proof of His love for you as His child? Explain.

_____

_____

_____

In truth, tribulations are, for those well prepared, like certain foods and exercises for athletes which lead the contestants on to glory, if, when reviled, we bless; if when maligned, we entreat; if ill-treated, we give thanks; if afflicted, we glory in our afflictions. It is indeed shameful for us to bless on propitious occasions but be silent on the dark and difficult ones. On the contrary, we must bless even more at that time, knowing that "The Lord disciplines him whom He loves and chastises every son who He receives."

Basil the Great (AD 330–379)

3

Conviction of Sin

2 Corinthians 7:2–12

Key Point

Godly sorrow through the conviction of sin leads to repentance without regret and to freedom in Christ.

Key Verse

Godly sorrow brings repentance that leads to salvation and leaves no regret, but worldly sorrow brings death.

2 Corinthians 7:10

Paul makes a distinction between godly sorrow for our sins and worldly sorrow in 2 Corinthians 7:9–11. Worldly sorrow can be due to a faulty conscience, the guilt trips we put on one another, or the accusations of the devil. We may feel guilty due to worldly sorrow, but that cannot change the fact that we are forgiven before God.

We all feel guilty when we violate our conscience. Our conscience is a function of our mind and will always be true to itself, but not necessarily to God. Our conscience was formed before we came to Christ as we assimilated values from our home, school, and social environments. Observing role models and learning right from wrong from others shaped our conscience, but human resources and role models are not infallible. When we come to Christ, our conscience changes as we are transformed by the renewing of our mind. Letting our conscience be our guide is not the same as letting the Holy Spirit be our guide.

Nonbelievers come under the conviction of sin and turn to Christ. "Godly sorrow brings repentance that leads to salvation and leaves no regret, but worldly sorrow brings death" (2 Corinthians 7:10). Should we sin as born-again believers, we will also have a sense of sorrow for what we have done. That is the convicting (not condemning) work of the Holy Spirit.

Worldly sorrow may feel the same as godly sorrow, but the end results are radically different. Many people are sorry they got caught sinning, but such sorrow seldom leads to repentance. Others may feel sorry for their sins and have an emotional catharsis and confess their sins to others. However, if there is no genuine repentance, they may regret this action later. Godly sorrow leads to repentance without regret. People don't regret finding their freedom in Christ through genuine repentance. They are thankful for their newfound freedom and sense no shame.

In a moment of crisis, Peter denied Christ three times (see Luke 22:60). However, he came under the conviction of the Holy Spirit, repented, and became the first spokesperson for the Early Church (see Luke 22:61–62; Acts 2:14–41). Judas also betrayed Jesus but succumbed to the sorrow of the world and hung himself (see Matthew 27:1–5). His actions did not demonstrate God-centered sorrow over the wickedness of sin that leads to death, but a self-centered sorrow over the temporal consequences of sin that had negatively affected him.

If you have been honest with God and yet struggle with condemning thoughts, rest assured that it is not God convicting you of sin. You first should consider by what standard you are evaluating your actions. Feeling guilty because you didn't carry on some family tradition is due to a faulty conscience. You also could be paying attention to a deceiving spirit. Paul wrote, "The Spirit clearly says that in later times some will abandon the faith and follow deceiving spirits and things taught by demons. Such teachings come through hypocritical liars, whose consciences have been seared as with a hot iron" (1 Timothy 4:1–2).

On Good Friday, one thief hung on a cross by Jesus and experienced the sorrow of the world and died, but the other "became sorrowful as God intended" (2 Corinthians 7:9) and joined Jesus in paradise (see Luke 23:40–43).

What is the distinction between godly sorrow for our sins and worldly sorrow?

What is the function of our conscience before we come to Christ? How does that change after we come to Christ?

Why are there no regrets after genuine repentance?

In what ways do you struggle with a guilty conscience?

Have you ever felt the conviction of sin and failed to repent? How did that work for you in the long run?

Paul was regretful before he saw the fruit of repentance, but afterward rejoiced. This is the nature of godly sorrow. Worldly sorrow, in contrast to this, is regret for the loss of money, reputation, and friends. That kind of sorrow merely leads to greater harm, because the regret is often a prelude to revenge. Only sorrow for sin is really profitable.

John Chrysostom (AD 347–407)

4

Our Inheritance in Christ
Hebrews 1:1–4

Key Point

Being a joint-heir with Jesus is every believer's birthright.

Key Verse

Now if we are children, then we are heirs—heirs of God and co-heirs with Christ, if indeed we share in his sufferings in order that we may also share in his glory.

Romans 8:17

God spoke to our forefathers through His prophets, but now He speaks to us through His Son (see Hebrews 1:1). Jesus is the ultimate revelation of God, as revealed by the seven following descriptive statements in verses 2–4 about Him. First, Jesus has been appointed heir of all things (see Romans 8:17). Second, through Jesus, the universe was made (see John 1:3; Colossians 1:18). Third, Jesus is the radiance of God's glory (see John 1:14, 18). Fourth, Jesus is the representation of the Father (see John 14:9; Colossians 1:15). Fifth, by His powerful word, Jesus sustains all things (see Colossians 1:17). Sixth, Jesus provided the purification of our sins (see Titus 2:14; Hebrews 7:27). Seventh, Jesus is seated at the right hand of the Majesty in heaven (see Hebrews 8:1; 10:12).

The destiny of Christians is bound up in the destiny of Jesus. "Christ has indeed been raised from the dead, the firstfruits of those who have [died]" (1 Corinthians 15:20). Jesus was the first to receive the birthright. As born-again believers, we also have a birthright because we are all children of God. "Now if we are children, then we are heirs—heirs of God and co-heirs with Christ" (Romans 8:17). All this is possible because we are spiritually alive "in Christ."

Paul writes, "God raised us up with Christ and seated us with him in the heavenly realms in Christ Jesus, in order that in the coming ages he might show the incomparable riches of his grace, expressed in his kindness to us in Christ Jesus" (Ephesians 2:6–7). As grateful believers we say, "Praise be to the God and Father of our Lord Jesus Christ, who has blessed us in the heavenly realms with every spiritual blessing in Christ" (1:3).

According to Ephesians 1:4–14, our inheritance in Christ includes being chosen in Christ before the creation of the world to be holy and blameless; predestined to be adopted as His sons and daughters through Jesus Christ; redeemed through Christ's blood, the forgiveness of sins; knowledgeable of the mystery of His will; chosen and predestined according to His plan; included in Christ when we heard the word of truth; and marked in Jesus with a seal, the promised Holy Spirit.

According to God's Word, we have a rich inheritance in Christ. The problem is that many Christians do not know it or fail to comprehend this incredible truth about being a joint heir with Jesus. So Paul prays that we would know God better and that our hearts would be enlightened in order that we may know the riches of our inheritance in Christ (see Ephesians 1:17–19). God's promises need to be claimed, and His truth needs to be believed in order for it to be effective in our lives.

As you close your study today, make this your prayer: "Glorious Father and God of my Lord and Savior Jesus Christ, I ask that You would give me the spirit of wisdom and revelation so that I may know You better. I pray also that the eyes of my heart may be enlightened in order that I may know the hope to which You have called me, the riches of Your glorious inheritance in the saints, and Your incomparably great power that You have extended to all of us who believe. In Jesus' name I pray. Amen."

Review Hebrews 1:1–4. What are some of the statements the author makes to show that Jesus is the ultimate revelation of God?

_____

_____

_____

_____

What have we received because we are a new creation in Christ? What has God promised to us since we are now co-heirs with Christ?

_____

_____

_____

According to Ephesians 1:4–14, what are some of the things our inheritance in Christ includes?

_____

_____

_____

Take a moment to reflect on your physical heritage in comparison to your spiritual inheritance. Can you explain the difference?

_____

_____

_____

What are the practical implications for knowing that you are a joint-heir with Christ?

How is it that He who died is always said to be the heir of life, when heirs are normally heirs of the dead? But of course Christ died in His humanity, not in His divinity. For with God, which is where our inheritance lies, the Father's gift is poured into His obedient children, so that one who is alive may be the heir of the Living One by his own merit and not by reason of death. . . . What it means to be a fellow heir with Christ we are taught by the apostle John, for among other things he says: "We know that when He appears we shall be like Him."

Ambrosiaster (written c. AD 366–384)

5

The Love of Christ

Ephesians 3:14–21

Key Point

God loves us not because we are lovable, but because it is His nature to love us.

Key Verse

I pray that the eyes of your heart may be enlightened in order that you may know the hope to which he has called you, the riches of his glorious inheritance in his holy people.

Ephesians 1:18

D oes God love us? If we performed better, would God love us more? Does God love one person more than another? Do we really know the rich inheritance that we have in Christ? Such questions trouble every defeated Christian.

Paul addresses these issues in the book of Ephesians by modeling how we should pray for all the saints—and possibly ourselves. Paul first prays that our knowledge of God would increase and that we would know the rich inheritance that we have in Christ (see Ephesians 1:17–18). Then, in

Ephesians 3:14–21, he asks that we be filled with the power to comprehend the love of Christ that goes beyond knowledge. He desires that all believers be rooted in the love of Christ, established and "filled to the measure of all the fullness of God" (verse 19).

The two dominant Greek words in Scripture translated as love are *agape* and *phileo*. *Phileo* is brotherly love. It represents the natural affection we show among family, friends, and countrymen. *Agape* is God's love. It reflects the nature of God, because "God is love" (1 John 4:16). God loves us not because we are lovable, but because it is His nature to love us. The love of God is not dependent on its object. That is why the love of God is unconditional.

It is imperative that, as a believer, you know that God loves you and why. If you performed better, God wouldn't love you any more than He does now. If you performed poorly, He would still love you the same. He may discipline you for your sake, "because the Lord disciplines the ones he loves" (Hebrews 12:6). Further, "If you are not disciplined—and everyone undergoes discipline—then you are illegitimate, not true sons and daughters at all" (Hebrews 12:8).

Jesus said, "A new command I give you: Love one another" (John 13:34). Before salvation, we loved one another as well as we humanly could. But with Christ in us, we have a new capacity to love because we have become a partaker of His divine nature (see 2 Peter 1:4). "We love because he first loved us" (1 John 4:19). Our ability to love others is due to the presence of God in our lives and is the measure of our maturity. Paul says, "The goal of this command is love, which comes from a pure heart and a good conscience and a sincere faith" (1 Timothy 1:5). As we grow in Christ, our nature takes on the nature of love and our capacity to love others increases.

To further your understanding of God's love, personalize Paul's prayer for yourself: "Heavenly Father, I pray that out of Your glorious riches You would strengthen me with power through Your Spirit in my inner being so that Christ may dwell in my heart through faith. I pray that I may be rooted and established in Your love. Grant me the power with all the saints to grasp how wide and long and high and deep is Your love. Enable me to know Your love that is beyond my mental ability to understand. Fill me to the measure of Your fullness. You are able to do immeasurably more than

I could ask or imagine, according to Your power that is at work within me. May You be glorified in Your Church throughout all generations forever and ever. Amen."

In Ephesians 3:14–21, how does Paul model how we should pray for ourselves and other believers in Christ?

_____

_____

_____

What does *phileo* love represent? What does *agape* love represent?

_____

_____

_____

Before we met Christ, we loved as much as we humanly could. What capacity do we now have to love after becoming partakers in Jesus' divine nature?

_____

_____

_____

Why does God love you? How do you know He does?

_____

_____

_____

Are there people in your life whom you struggle to love? Does that struggle have more to do with you or the other person? Explain.

_____

_____

_____

The text "God so loved the world," shows such an intensity of love. For great indeed and infinite is the distance between the two. The immortal, the infinite majesty without beginning or end loved those who were but dust and ashes, who were loaded with ten thousand sins but remained ungrateful even as they constantly offended Him. This is who He "loved." For God did not give a servant, or an angel or even an archangel "but His only begotten Son."

John Chrysostom (AD 347–407)

Leader's Tips

The following are some guidelines for leaders to follow when using the VICTORY SERIES studies with a small group. Generally, the ideal size for a group is between 10 and 20 people, which is small enough for meaningful fellowship but large enough for dynamic group interaction. It is typically best to stop opening up the group to members after the second session and invite them to join the next study after the six weeks are complete.

Structuring Your Time Together

For best results, ensure that all participants have a copy of the book. They should be encouraged to read the material and consider the questions and applications on their own before the group session. If participants have to miss a meeting, they should keep abreast of the study on their own. The group session reinforces what they learned and offers the valuable perspectives of others. Learning best takes place in the context of committed relationships, so do more than just share answers. Take the time to care and share with one another. You might want to use the first week to distribute material and give everyone a chance to tell others who they are.

If you discussed just one topic a week, it would take several years to finish the VICTORY SERIES. If you did five a week, it is possible to complete the whole series in 48 weeks. All the books in the series were written with a six-week study in mind. However, each group is different and each will have to discover its own pace. If too many participants come unprepared, you may have to read, or at least summarize, the text before discussing the questions and applications.

It would be great if this series was used for a church staff or Bible study at work and could be done one topic at a time, five days a week. However, most study groups will likely be meeting weekly. It is best to start with a time of sharing and prayer for one another. Start with the text or Bible passage for each topic and move to the discussion questions and application. Take time at the end to summarize what has been covered, and dismiss in prayer.

Group Dynamics

Getting a group of people actively involved in discussing critical issues of the Christian life is very rewarding. Not only does group interaction help to create interest, stimulate thinking, and encourage effective learning, but it is also vital for building quality relationships within the group. Only as people begin to share their thoughts and feelings will they begin to build bonds of friendship and support.

It is important to set some guidelines at the beginning of the study, as follows:

- There are no wrong questions.
- Everyone should feel free to share his or her ideas without recrimination.
- Focus on the issues and not on personalities.
- Try not to dominate the discussions or let others do so.
- Personal issues shared in the group must remain in the group.
- Avoid gossiping about others in or outside the group.
- Side issues should be diverted to the end of the class for those who wish to linger and discuss them further.
- Above all, help each other grow in Christ.

Some may find it difficult to share with others, and that is okay. It takes time to develop trust in any group. A leader can create a more open and sharing atmosphere by being appropriately vulnerable himself or herself. A good leader doesn't have all the answers and doesn't need to for this study. Some questions raised are extremely difficult to answer and have been puzzled over for years by educated believers. We will never have all the answers to every question in this age, but that does not preclude discussion over eternal matters. Hopefully, it will cause some to dig deeper.

Leading the Group

The following tips can be helpful in making group interaction a positive learning opportunity for everyone:

- When a question or comment is raised that is off the subject, suggest that you will bring it up again at the end of the class if anyone is still interested.

- When someone talks too much, direct a few questions specifically to other people, making sure not to put any shy people on the spot. Talk privately with the "dominator" and ask for cooperation in helping to draw out the quieter group members.

- Hopefully the participants have already written their answers to the discussion questions and will share that when asked. If most haven't come prepared, give them some time to personally reflect on what has been written and the questions asked.

- If someone asks a question that you don't know how to answer, admit it and move on. If the question calls for insight about personal experience, invite group members to comment. If the question requires specialized knowledge, offer to look for an answer before the next session. (Make sure to follow up the next session.)

- When group members disagree with you or each other, remind them that it is possible to disagree without becoming disagreeable. To help clarify the issues while maintaining a climate of mutual acceptance, encourage those on opposite sides to restate what they have heard the other person(s) saying about the issue. Then invite each side to evaluate how accurately they feel their position was presented. Ask group members to identify as many points as possible related to the topic on which both sides agree, and then lead the group in examining

157

other Scriptures related to the topic, looking for common ground that they can all accept.

- Finally, urge group members to keep an open heart and mind and a willingness to continue loving one another while learning more about the topic at hand.

If the disagreement involves an issue on which your church has stated a position, be sure that stance is clearly and positively presented. This should be done not to squelch dissent but to ensure that there is no confusion over where your church stands.

Notes

Session Five

Chapter 4 A New Heart

1. H. Wheeler Robinson, *The Christian Doctrine of Man* (Edinburgh, Scotland: T & T Clark, 1926), p. 22.

Victory Series Scope
and Sequence Overview

The Victory Series is composed of eight studies that create a comprehensive discipleship course. Each study builds on the previous one and provides six sessions of material. These can be used by an individual or in a small group setting. There are leader's tips at the back of each study for those leading a small group.

The following scope and sequence overview gives a brief summary of the content of each of the eight studies in the Victory Series. Some studies also include articles related to the content of that study.

The Victory Series

Study 1   God's Story for You: Discover the Person God Created You to Be

---

Session One: The Story of Creation
Session Two: The Story of the Fall
Session Three: The Story of Salvation
Session Four: The Story of God's Sanctification
Session Five: The Story of God's Transforming Power
Session Six: The Story of God

Study 2   Your New Identity: A Transforming Union With God

Session One: A New Life "in Christ"
Session Two: A New Understanding of God's Character
Session Three: A New Understanding of God's Nature
Session Four: A New Relationship With God
Session Five: A New Humanity
Session Six: A New Beginning

Study 3   Your Foundation in Christ: Live by the Power of the Spirit

---

Session One: Liberating Truth
Session Two: The Nature of Faith
Session Three: Living Boldly
Session Four: Godly Relationships
Session Five: Freedom of Forgiveness
Session Six: Living by the Spirit

Study 4   Renewing Your Mind: Become More Like Christ

Session One: Being Transformed
Session Two: Living Under Grace
Session Three: Overcoming Anger
Session Four: Overcoming Anxiety
Session Five: Overcoming Depression
Session Six: Overcoming Losses

Coming Soon

Study 5   Growing in Christ: Deepen Your Relationship With Jesus

---

Session One: Spiritual Discernment
Session Two: Spiritual Gifts
Session Three: Growing Through Committed Relationships
Session Four: Overcoming Sexual Bondage
Session Five: Overcoming Chemical Addiction
Session Six: Suffering for Righteousness' Sake

Study 6   Your Life in Christ: Walk in Freedom by Faith

Session One: God's Will
Session Two: Faith Appraisal (Part 1)
Session Three: Faith Appraisal (Part 2)
Session Four: Spiritual Leadership
Session Five: Discipleship Counseling
Session Six: The Kingdom of God

Study 7 Your Authority in Christ: Overcoming the Enemy

Session One: The Origin of Evil
Session Two: God and Evil Spirits
Session Three: Overcoming the Opposition
Session Four: Kingdom Sovereignty
Session Five: The Armor of God (Part 1)
Session Six: The Armor of God (Part 2)

Study 8   Your Ultimate Victory: Standing Strong in the Faith

Session One: The Battle for Our Minds
Session Two: The Lure of Knowledge and Power
Session Three: Overcoming Temptation
Session Four: Overcoming Accusation
Session Five: Overcoming Deception
Session Six: Degrees of Spiritual Vulnerability

Books and Resources
Dr. Neil T. Anderson

Core Material

Victory Over the Darkness with study guide, audiobook, and DVD. With over 1,300,000 copies in print, this core book explains who you are in Christ, how to walk by faith in the power of the Holy Spirit, how to be transformed by the renewing of your mind, how to experience emotional freedom, and how to relate to one another in Christ.

The Bondage Breaker with study guide, audiobook, and DVD. With over 1,300,000 copies in print, this book explains spiritual warfare, what our protection is, ways that we are vulnerable, and how we can live a liberated life in Christ.

Breaking Through to Spiritual Maturity. This curriculum teaches the basic message of Freedom in Christ Ministries.

Discipleship Counseling with DVD. This book combines the concepts of discipleship and counseling and teaches the practical integration of theology and psychology for helping Christians resolve their personal and spiritual conflicts through repentance and faith in God.

Steps to Freedom in Christ and interactive video. This discipleship counseling tool helps Christians resolve their personal and spiritual conflicts through genuine repentance and faith in God.

Restored. This book is an expansion of the *Steps to Freedom in Christ*, and offers more explanation and illustrations.

Walking in Freedom. This book is a 21-day devotional that we use for follow-up after leading someone through the Steps to Freedom.

Freedom in Christ is a discipleship course for Sunday school classes and small groups. The course comes with a teacher's guide, a student guide, and a DVD covering 12 lessons and the Steps to Freedom in Christ. This course is designed to enable new and stagnant believers to resolve personal and spiritual conflicts and be established alive and free in Christ.

The Bondage Breaker DVD Experience is also a discipleship course for Sunday School classes and small groups. It is similar to the one above, but the lessons are 15 minutes instead of 30 minutes.

The Daily Discipler. This practical systematic theology is a culmination of all of Dr. Anderson's books covering the major doctrines of the Christian faith and the problems Christians face. It is a five-day-per-week, one-year study that will thoroughly ground believers in their faith.

Specialized Books

The Bondage Breaker, the Next Step. This book has several testimonies of people finding their freedom from all kinds of problems, with commentary by Dr. Anderson. It is an important learning tool for encouragers.

Overcoming Addictive Behavior, with Mike Quarles. This book explores the path to addiction and how a Christian can overcome addictive behaviors.

Overcoming Depression, with Joanne Anderson. This book explores the nature of depression, which is a body, soul, and spirit problem and presents a wholistic answer for overcoming this "common cold" of mental illness.

Liberating Prayer. This book helps believers understand the confusion in their minds when it comes time to pray, and why listening in prayer may be more important than talking.

Daily in Christ, with Joanne Anderson. This popular daily devotional is also being used by thousands of Internet subscribers every day.

Who I Am in Christ. In 36 short chapters, this book describes who you are in Christ and how He meets your deepest needs.

Freedom from Addiction, with Mike and Julia Quarles. Using Mike's testimony, this book explains the nature of chemical addictions and how to overcome them in Christ.

One Day at a Time, with Mike and Julia Quarles. This devotional helps those who struggle with addictive behaviors and explains how to discover the grace of God on a daily basis.

Freedom from Fear, with Rich Miller. This book explains anxiety disorders and how to overcome them.

Setting Your Church Free, with Charles Mylander. This book offers guidelines and encouragement for resolving seemingly impossible corporate conflicts in the church and also provides leaders with a primary means for church growth—releasing the power of God in the church.

Setting Your Marriage Free, with Dr. Charles Mylander. This book explains God's divine plan for marriage and the steps that couples can take to resolve their difficulties.

Christ-Centered Therapy, with Dr. Terry and Julie Zuehlke. This is a textbook explaining the practical integration of theology and psychology for professional counselors.

Getting Anger Under Control, with Rich Miller. This book explains the basis for anger and how to control it.

Grace that Breaks the Chains, with Rich Miller and Paul Travis. This book explains legalism and how to overcome it.

Winning the Battle Within. This book shares God's standards for sexual conduct, the path to sexual addiction, and how to overcome sexual strongholds.

The Path to Reconciliation. God has given the church the ministry of reconciliation. This book explains what that is and how it can be accomplished.

Rough Road to Freedom. This is a book of Dr. Anderson's memoirs.

For more information, contact Freedom In Christ Ministries at the following:

Canada: freedominchrist@sasktel.net or www.ficm.ca

India: isactara@vsnl.com

Switzerland: info@freiheitinchristus.ch or www.freiheitinchristus.ch

United Kingdom: info@ficm.org.uk or www.ficm.org.uk

United States: info@ficm.org or www.ficm.org

International: www.ficminternational.org

Dr. Anderson: www.discipleshipcounsel.com

Index

Dr. Neil T. Anderson was formerly the chairman of the Practical Theology Department at Talbot School of Theology. In 1989, he founded Freedom in Christ Ministries, which now has staff and offices in various countries around the world. He is currently on the Freedom in Christ Ministries International Board, which oversees this global ministry. For more information about Dr. Anderson and his ministry, visit his website at www.ficminternational.org.

Also From
Neil T. Anderson

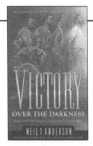

This bestselling landmark book gives you practical, productive ways to discover who you are in Christ. When you realize the power of your true identity, you can shed the burdens of your past, stand against evil influences, and become the person Christ empowers you to be.

Victory Over the Darkness

Great for small group or individual use, these thought-provoking personal reflection questions and applications for each chapter of *Victory Over the Darkness* will help readers grow in the strength and truth of their powerful identity in Jesus Christ.

Victory Over the Darkness Study Guide

BETHANYHOUSE

Stay up-to-date on your favorite books and authors with our free e-newsletters. Sign up today at bethanyhouse.com.

Find us on Facebook. facebook.com/BHPnonfiction

Follow us on Twitter. @bethany_house

16071721R00099

Printed in Great Britain
by Amazon